Pioneer German Sisters

The Real Missionaries of the Pacific "Wild" West

Inga Jablonsky

Lulu.com

With love and gratitude for my most ardent supporter, Bill.

If J.F. Kennedy were still around and would want to write a sequel to his book *Profiles in Courage*, he could, if he had met the Poor School Sisters of St. Dominic who labored in the Pacific Northwest for so many years. He could title it *The Pioneer Dominican Sisters*, because he would realize that the spirit of courage, sacrifice and love dominated them. You can see that this still shines forth in the few that are left of the group. That's my salute to the Dominican nuns.

— Sister Padraig

Preface

This book presents the history of the German Dominican Sisters, now in Spokane, Washington. Since I came to know about the Sisters' existence, in 1995, their story has fascinated me. I learned that between 1925 and 1937, sixty-four young German women came to Kettle Falls, Washington - to the Pacific Northwest - to build hospitals and schools and to adopt the work of the Indian Mission in Omak, Washington.

In this book, the *Poor School Sisters* will speak for themselves. The material has been collected from the authorized records of the Spokane Dominican archives to include specifically:

- *Journal of the Early Days*, as recorded by Mother M. Bonaventura, 1925
- transcripts of 18 interviews with the German sisters from 1975, recorded on audio tapes
- personal accounts, written within the Dominican Order
- journal entries in either German or English, recorded at the Dominican archives, Spokane
- the Dominican brochure: *A Measure of Leaven*

- *Community History, Vol. I*
- Photographic records

Also, Sr. Ilma Raufer's publication, *Black Robes and Indians on the Last Frontier*, needs to be credited for some of the historic references used in this book.

I am responsible for collecting the material, selecting the documents to be included, transcribing the audiotapes, translating all German documents into English, and arranging everything in sequence for the history of the Poor School Sisters to shine through clearly. I also made an effort to preserve German-specific language patters in hopes for the reader to genuinely perceive their voices. What I aimed for and am most pleased about is that this book contains only pure and true historical content.

This history proposes a true account, in word and photography, of religious women pioneers in the Pacific Northwest, with special attention given to their work with Native Americans. It will also portray individual women living with their families in Nazi Germany, their leaving for the New World, and the ravages and horrors that were inflicted by the Hitler Regime and during war times on everybody they left behind.

In honor of Mother Bonaventura specifically, the German Dominican Sisters still in Spokane, Washington, or Sinsinawa, Wisconsin, and all Sisters everywhere.

Contents

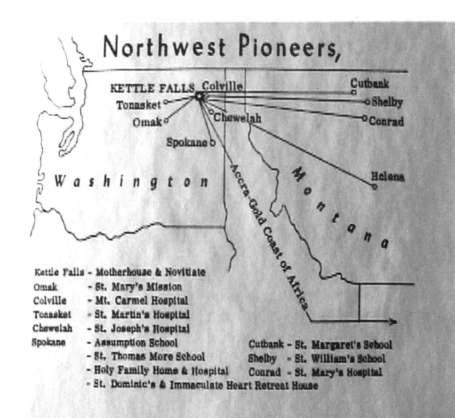

Northwest Pioneers,

KETTLE FALLS Colville
Tonasket
Omak
Chewelah
Spokane

Cutbank
Shelby
Conrad

Washington

Accra Gold Coast of Africa

Montana

Helena

Kettle Falls – Motherhouse & Novitiate
Omak   – St. Mary's Mission
Colville   – Mt. Carmel Hospital
Tonasket   – St. Martin's Hospital
Chewelah – St. Joseph's Hospital
Spokane   – Assumption School
          – St. Thomas More School
          – Holy Family Home & Hospital
          – St. Dominic's & Immaculate Heart Retreat House

Cutbank – St. Margaret's School
Shelby – St. William's School
Conrad – St. Mary's Hospital

Introduction:

Traveling the Roads of the Past:
From Spokane to Chewelah, Washington

I'm trying so hard to see everything through their eyes. *S ch' wee la* on a terracotta brown rock slab nestled in the grass near a wooden hut with the inscription: *St. Francis Regis Mission of the Crees.* Was that already there when they came here?

St. Francis Regis: I remember that name. In 1934, Mother Bonaventura wrote about it. "... We believe to have found a suitable place in the Colville Sisters' old boarding school for girls just opposite the historic Jesuit Mission of St. Regis."

The framed legend nailed to the door of the hut explains:

AT THE BEGINNING of the 19th century
mixed blood Cree and French-speaking Métis free traders
crossed the Rocky Mountains at the Athabasca Pass.
They found a home among the Salish speaking peoples,
and settled in the villages of the Colville Valley.
Pierre-Jean DeSmet, S.J., 1845

We're in Chewelah, the first station of my journey back into the Poor School Sisters' American history. I want to visit St. Mary of the Pines, the farm that Mother Bonaventura and her twenty German sisters bought in March of 1931.

It wasn't a glorious late summer day then, no golden wheat fields in abundance, and the farmhouse in a state of disrepair. But I can feel the spirit of the young German women in this place, or is it my own spirit in a country that is as different to me as it was to them? There are many *Bauernhöfe* – farms – in Germany, but their fields certainly don't stretch to the horizon, nor is the horizon even visible. The land there is so much smaller, narrower.

The car turns around when the road ends in the middle of the farm grounds. I think I can recognize one of the old buildings in back as the original farm building. They were so poor.

It was so poor, there was nothing there. Just a big hall and no divisions, no table, the only things were in our trunk. We did not have any bedside table. We did not have any closet. We had only our bed. We took two apple boxes together and put our wash pans on top and put our shoes under. We had no chair; nothing was there. The clothes were hanging on the pipes. We really cried because it was very great poverty, and we were not used to this.

But all the crying is done at night; during the day they band together in work, prayer, singing and laughter. They are young, and they only speak German. I am trying to feel close to them, although I cannot imagine being so poor and working so hard. But I am a pioneer also, coming to a foreign country. A woman, also. A teacher, like many of the sisters. And German.

The Beginnings

Mother Bonaventura's Diary, 1925

In nomine Domine!
Convent St. Mary Magdalena,
12. August 1925

O n August 12th, 1925, in the evening at 7 o'clock, tweleve sisters from the motherhouse of the *Institute of the Poor School Sisters of the Third Order of Penance of St. Dominic* in Speyer on the Rhine River – Rhineland-Palatinate, Germany – arrived in Helena, Montana, to establish the first American foundation in order to take care of the domestic affairs in Mount St. Charles College there.

How did school sisters from Speyer end up in the far away Helena in the "Wild West"? Through God's special foreordination.

The Beginnings

It was in the evening of December 28th, in the year of the Lord 1923, when His Excellency, the Most Reverend Dr. Ludwig Sebastian, Bishop of Speyer, the glorious imperial city, came to our motherhouse to greet our Reverend Mother, Prioress M. Aquinata Steinfeltz, with the following words:

"Mother Prioress, I came to you today with a request. And please don't say no. His Excellency, the Most Reverend John Carroll, Bishop of Helena, Montana, in the United States has asked me in a letter to send sisters to attend to the domestic affairs in his boarding school for boys, *Mount St. Charles College.*"

The Reverend Mother understood the bishop's plea as an order from God, and in her mind she said, "Yes", trusting in the never-ending benevolence of the Divine providence. But she asked His Excellency, the Bishop, for some time to think it over with her Lord and the council. In the end, all council sisters acknowledged the call as coming from God, and Mother Aquinata gave the bishop her and the council's consent.

At once, negotiations commenced with His Excellency, the Bishop of Helena, who was full of joy over the gracious obligingness of the Speyer bishop. Mother Aquinata approved the desired number of twelve sisters for the college with one condition: that His Excellency, the Bishop, would in time assign the sisters for school service, since teaching the female youth was the main objective of the Institute of the Poor School Sisters. His Graciousness readily granted the request with the endorsement: "that the sisters have to remain at the college indefinitely."

The sisters in the Motherhouse started to look critically and doubtfully towards an emigration of some of their own to a foreign country abroad – until now they had only been working within their home diocese in Speyer. Both within the community of the sisters and in the clergy there were a lot of difficult pros and cons and times were hard for Mother Aquinata. But supported and encouraged by a few broad-minded men, among them Monsignor Richard Schaefer, chaplain of the community; Albert Meckes, professor of theology and most ardent supporter of the cause; and Rev. Muenchen, S.J., spiritual director of the community, she bravely overcame all resistance and kept to her "Yes", asking only for the Lord's help.

It was time to appoint the sisters, and Mother Prioress requested those sisters prepared for emigration to volunteer. A number of sisters responded to the appeal of the Reverend Mother. From among those, Mother Aquinata and her council chose the ones to go. The day and the hour of the departure had already been set, when an unforeseen complication arose. Was this in destiny's plan?

On July 1ˢᵗ, 1924, the new immigration laws of the United States had been changed to also include nuns in the existing quota. Nuns or anyone in the clergy had previously been exempted under the Immigration Act, and the sisters were advised to wait until the year 1927. Enthusiasm for the new foundation began to wane and the limitations of the new Immigration Act were considered seriously. Upon Mother Aquinata's request, Bishop Sebastian sent a cancellation letter to Bishop Carroll. The dear bishop, deeply disappointed in his joy and hope, renewed his efforts to obtain travel permits for the sisters. Reverend Father G. Fimpe, S.J., General Secretary of the St. Raphael Society in Hamburg, entered into negotiations with the American embassy in Frankfurt.

Everyone abandoned their expectations, only Mother Aquinata hoped against all hope. It was her most ardent desire to have Dominican foundations abroad. In Helena, Bishop Carroll had already built a house for the sisters and had made grave sacrifices.

Thanks to the efforts of Reverend P. Fimpe, the American consulate in Frankfurt promised greatest consideration to the sisters, and – finally - in July 1925, eleven sisters received an entry visa for America. Their names were: Sister Bonaventura Groh [the writer of this diary], Sister Arsenia Stalter, Sister Walburgis Mayer, Sister Virginia Mathieu, Sister Eugenia Schneider, Sister Gallena Klomann, Sister Gisela German, Sister Jukunda

Eichenlaub, Sister Klodia Joerg, Sister Mitis Weißenmayer and Postulant Hedwig Friebe (postulant: candidate for admission).

Last preparations had to be made. The entire diocese participated in the events at the Institute of the Poor School Sisters in Speyer. Those were hard times, especially for parents, siblings and other relatives of the chosen sisters. But even they said their *"Fiat!"* – "It shall happen" – and made their sacrifice of parting, albeit with a heavy heart.

On Sunday, July 26, 1925, in the octave of the feast of St. Mary Magdalena, patron saint of the Dominican Order, in the afternoon at 3 o'clock, there was a small farewell celebration in the gym of the dear motherhouse. Mother M. Bonaventura was appointed superior of the group. Monsignor Schaefer compared with articulate and stirring words our sea travel with that of Lazarus, Martha and Maria Magdalena, when they were driven into exile in a rudderless boat. One Lazarus, His Excellency the Bishop of Speyer, sent us, and a second Lazarus, His Excellency the Bishop of Helena, called for us. And under the wonderful protection of the Holy Martha and Mary Magdalena we embarked on our journey.

Relatives of the sisters and friends of the convent participated in the celebration. With witty words and moving song, our Reverend Mother Prioress and all sisters said their farewells and expressed their most heartfelt wishes for us on our journey.

On July 27, 1925, the day had come to say goodbye. After a going-away coffee in the assembly room of the convent, where the sisters summoned up their everything, good-byes had to be said to our dear Savior in the oh so familiar, dear little chapel. After exposure of the Blessed Sacrament and a few glorious hymns, we said the prayers prescribed by the Dominican Order for those departing for missions in foreign lands. Then we renewed our vows, followed by the Benediction of the Blessed Sacrament. For our Blessed Lord we were going to leave our parents and siblings, our convent family and our native land. A last good-bye to the beloved motherhouse and all our dear fellow sisters, and away we went. The little bell of the convent tower rang out in greetings of farewell as we pilgrims left for the train station.

The Poor School Sisters' Voices

What were the thoughts of the Poor School Sisters? Their reasons and expectations and many other memories and thoughts of their emigration were documented in recorded interviews on their 50th anniversary in the U.S., 1975. Their voices are as diffcrent from each other as all human reflections and undertakings are. With the exception of Mother Bonaventura's memories, the thoughts of the original eleven travelers, the brave souls who led the way, are missing. The others remember various years of U.S. emigrations, different travels and callings. The Second World War only set an end for a while to the sisters' emigration.

In their interviews, the sisters report of their anguished partings throughout the years: mothers and fathers, brothers and sisters, left behind to possibly never be seen again.

Sister Coelestine, 1928: The postulants gave us a farewell party in the big hall in Speyer. Our relatives were there. My mother was there; my father just died in April. Otherwise I couldn't have made it. I couldn't have talked him into going along. But my mother wanted to say her good byes, so oh: everyone was crying their eyes out. We ate a nice meal in the motherhouse. We left with a farewell blessing and then we left for the train. We walked out. Someone brought our trunks out. I mean, it was all taken care of. And then we went to the train and when I was sitting in the train, I looked out of the window. And there were my brother and my sister, smiling. They just came; they went on the Sunday before I left just to see me -- oh, I'll never forget that. It sure picked me up.

So we went to Mannheim by train, and then Mother and Aunt Bernarda went on the train along to Mannheim. And then in the evening we left by train to Bremen. On the way, Sister Humilia had a big sausage she brought from home. But we had no bread and so we ate pound cake with it, I'll never forget. It didn't taste too good, but oh, we were hungry. And that night we slept in Bremen. We had to stay all night. And they had beds made with feather duvets, and I'll never forget, I liked them so well because I never could fix our featherbeds so nice. You'd have to be tall, I guess. I liked it very much. So it was my first joy, those nice beds.

Sister Francis deSales, 1933: When the firsts sisters left for America we were all standing in front of the convent waving good-bye, singing a song, and they were crying.

Unidentified Voices: I have to tell you what happened in Speyer. We were standing in hooded gowns before we went, and suddenly I said, what am I doing? I don't want to go through with this. I don't want to do this, and my mother just took my hand and I looked around to see where I should go. And then she pushed me into the chapel: it must be the will of God. And then, when we got on the train, I thought, it will be all right.

I still remember that pain when we went on the bus and my mother put her arms around me. That was so hard. You felt like you were going to die, it was such a pain. Our mothers went along and when they left I felt... oh... remember how the one sister cried? When I left, my mother hugged me so tight and said, " My only child, my girl, is going to leave me now." I thought I couldn't go. This is it, I can't go. Mother came with me until Neukirchen. My dad went. I never saw my mother again.

Their Vocation

It was so hard to say good-bye. How did the Poor School Sisters get through this? The reasons were their commitment to the Lord and their strong devotion. The sisters were willing to make any kind of sacrifices. Hardworking, dedicated and prayerful, with just a kind of common, ordinary sense of duty and dedication to duty, they would work out their commitment to serve. They were always cheerful and joyous, even when their days were much harder than those of any others.

Sister Catherine, 1933: We see each other as persons, try to see what's in us. Respect and love let us discover a new meaning in each other. That we accept. There is a greater openness. It's amazing how much we can give each other if we listen to each other. See, when you succeed, even when you're tired from a day's work, you are together. You support and strengthen each other and you start to talk about something and you forget about your tiredness.

Sister Mary Magdalene, 1937: The service for others is so important. It makes me happy and at the mission, too, when I saw the children. And just to see the children walk in the dining room, and the look on their faces when there was something good on the table, that was the biggest thank you expected.

Sister Imelda, 1938: The simplicity is very beautiful in our community.

Unidentified Voices: It's nice to help other people, if you are able to, help them and see that they come close to God. It's the nicest thing. It's nice to talk about God. It's the most challenging thing, and I always enjoy doing it. I love the community. I feel at home and I love the sisters. It's a place of God. There are special qualities of simplicity and our openness, our friendliness and concern, I think, for humanity.

I love our friendliness and our openness and our hospitality. I often said, in the Middle Ages, the convents were like hotels. Where everybody went for food and drink and shelter, and whenever an epidemic broke out, who were the ones to help? It was the priests, the nuns, and the monks who took in the sick, the travelers. It was always the convents. I always think, we can never be hospitable enough. I believe in a lot of goodness so that there is always an open house to everybody, no matter who it is, no matter what religion he has, what beliefs he has, what background he has. We are always open to anyone who comes and wants to share our life. I like that part, that we also try to understand each other, the old, the young – the young, the old.

Reasons for Leaving

Sister Xavier, 1937: Why did I come to the United States? They had sisters teaching at school. How I loved to teach! And the possibility of working at a mission was also given. Why shouldn't I sacrifice a lot to this goal of being a missionary?

Sister Benigna, 1937: We thought it was regular mission work. It was sort of an adventure, too, to come over here, to go to a mission. We thought it was all Indians, all Indian Territory, to go to mission, like you go to Africa or China or anyplace else.

Sister Fidelis, 1937: I came because there was no future in Germany during Hitler's time. There was no future for me, for anyone whose parent worked for the government, and my dad worked for the railroad. And in Germany the railroad is run by the government. So I wouldn't have to stay on the continent, that is my reason for coming over here, and there is also a strong tradition of missionary work in my dad's family. There have been missionaries for some time, so always I have had a great desire to go to the missions, and at that time we thought America was running wild with Indians, so when we came over here, we really didn't know what we would come to.

Sister Marina, 1928: Well, I wanted to be a missionary, that's all. My older sister was a missionary in South America, and I wanted to be a missionary, too, so I was the first one to volunteer.

Unidentified Voices: For us America meant a colony of Indians. We thought Chicago was uncivilized and was Indian country.

Permissions

Sister Eumelia, 1932: I was asked to get permission from my parents to come to the United States. And I said, they would never give permission to come to the United States. I was to write home anyway. So I wrote home. Mother wrote back and she said, "We are not going to give you permission but do what you think is right."

Sister Benigna, 1937: I wanted to go very badly, but my dad had died, so my mother was alone and I had only one brother, only the two of us. And she said, "As long as you belong to me I won't let you go." So, well, I forgot about the whole thing. So Mother Bonaventura wrote to Speyer again and asked if there weren't any young people interested to come to America to help them because there were only the few over there. They wanted to start hospitals. And so word went around and I thought, well, I want to go; I really want to go. And I prayed. And I went home, and my mother met me at the railroad station. We walked home. She had coffee ready for me, and I couldn't wait. I said, "Mutter, remember how years ago you wouldn't let me go to America; would you let me go now?" And she said yes. That was really, really the answer to my prayer. That was really a big sacrifice on my mom's part because I was the only girl; my brother was younger. There wasn't anybody else at home. And I told her,

"Don't come with me to Hamburg," I said, "I just couldn't take it." It was enough to say goodbye at home and she hugged me so tight. And at that moment I thought I couldn't go. So she went with me. We had two weeks before we left.

Sister Isentrude, 1937: They had too many sisters then, and they gave us a choice to go home or come over here. So I was the first one who said, I want to go. And Mother Superior said if the doctor lets you go and if you pass the exam, health wise, I have nothing against it. So I wrote to my parents, and I had to ask for permission, but I didn't ask. I said, "I'm to go to America and I want your okay" to my parents because I was the oldest of six girls and I thought they will miss me for a little while and then they won't miss me anymore. They had five more. So I had no trouble and, on the way over, they were all sick except me. I also took care of everybody when we came to the motherhouse on the 14th of August '37. Then I was sick for a few days and I worried they would send me home again and Mother Bonaventura said, "You don't have to worry, we would never send you home anymore."

Unidentified Voices: Because our community was not founded as a mission community, everyone who left needed their parents' permission to go. And then came the time of Hitler. It looked like all the Catholic schools were losing their nun teachers. That is the only reason why my father finally gave me permission to go. My father started teaching himself, and he saw the signs of the time. And only because of this did I finally get permission to go.

What They Left Behind

Germany is at the beginning of a downward spiral that would lead to disaster and the Holocaust. Here's what the sisters left behind:

Munich, 1925. The NSDAP - National Socialist German Workers' Party - has been newly founded and restructured: then Reich President Friedrich Ebert dies. The sharpest polemics, demagogy and defamations are the climate of the times, and the NSDAP is a nest of evil. There, on November 9, the SS *Schutzstaffel* - protection league - is born. Together with the SA *Sturmabteilung* - storm troop - with Hermann Göring as a commander, these most terrifying combat troops in uniform bully and violate the country and those of its citizens that are described by the party's philosophy as unworthy: Jewish people, communists, social democrats, homosexuals, handicapped people and anybody who sympathizes with or tries to assist these groups.

Are the dangers and anxieties of daily life the reasons for the German parents to ship their young daughters off to the new world? Can they foresee what most Germans cannot? But the sisters only have memories of their home lives:

Unidentified voices: My father, he had a big study with his desk just so, with a lot of books in English, but everything in the house had to be organized in order. You could never touch his desk because he knew exactly where he had things, and he could tell. I never heard him say, "Where did I put that?" Maybe later, when he got older. I was 23 when I left, so he was 53. We were exactly 30 years apart. I only knew him up to 53. But I don't know if he lapsed when he got older. I suppose he did. But I didn't experience it. He loved teaching, too.

I loved music, and we had a lot of music at home. We had a piano, an organ, a mandolin. My father used to teach all these instruments, and he started a band with the school children, and that's how these instruments came in our house. This was really a family affair: singing and playing music. And I remember, as a child, my father used to call us Sunday mornings, and he used to play the violin in front of the bedroom door, or at times he played

the piano and would sing when I took a nap. We played music a
lot, and we sang a lot. We always did this in church, too, as little
kids trying to read the psalms, and then when it was the vespers. I
remember I would always ask, what psalms do we sing? I love
music, and I was glad to teach.

Church of St. Joseph, Speyer, 1920

View onto the Kaiser Dome, Speyer

The Old Imperial City of Speyer

Kaiser Dome in Speyer, seen from the Rhine River

Institute of the Poor School Sisters of St. Dominic

On Board of MS "Deutschland"

The New Home Beckons

The Journey

Different kinds of sea travel would take place throughout the years, in good weather and bad.

The Good

Sister Marina, 1928: Oh, we had a very, very, very pleasant journey. We had the most pleasant weather, the captain said, for months and months, and he contributed it to us 12 Dominican sisters and 20 Franciscan sisters. They traveled north on a mission and eight priests and a bishop went to South America, but the bishop was in New York with us, and he said Mass for us on Sunday and he liked us Dominicans.

In the evening we went to the bow of the ship and we stood there. We had all good voices. We were young sisters then, and we sang all kinds of German songs, and as soon as we started we had a whole audience around us, and they all listened and clapped their hands and told us to go on singing, go on, sing more, sing more. They enjoyed it so much.

Sister Eumelia, 1932: Oh, we enjoyed the journey. We never got sick, in fact they bet money on us because we never got sick and never missed a meal and we had lots of fun.

The Bad

Sister Birgitta, 1928: It was one of the small ships, only for 200 persons. The trip lasted 7 days. The first days were nice; oh, they were nice on deck chairs. There were chairs in the sunshine. When the storm came, we were all sick. The storm was terrific, the worst the captain experienced in his 36 years at sea. He summoned all the passengers to the dining room and told us, when it came to the worst, which ways to go. Nothing could happen to us. We were ten sisters. We were praying and singing; we sang every evening. And more and more passengers came to listen to us. Every evening seasickness, and we sang every evening and then of course the singing stopped. After the storm, nobody could go on deck. Every hole was closed. Our ship was like a nutshell on the waves. Nobody in the dining room anymore. When the storm started, the attendants poured water on the tablecloths so the dishes wouldn't move but nobody was in the dining room anymore, except Sisters Marina and Cornelia. The storm was seven or eight days. We felt like our ship stood still in the ocean, and we wondered what happened. Well, we ventured out, and there were icebergs. Oh, it was beautiful to see. Icebergs full of seagulls. Came down from Greenland, but icebergs are 1/3 only above the water and 2/3 below the water. And the danger to the ship: once an iceberg had cut a ship in two. So we stood still in the ocean. But it was beautiful to see. And we had to wait, the navigator had to watch how the icebergs moved, before we could move, so we had two days longer on board than we were supposed to have. During the storm, most of the passengers spent that time in bed, being sick. The last three days on the ocean were beautiful. We had concerts: the ship's band played every day. We were lying on deck enjoying the good air and sunshine. We got our coffee, we got our bouillon, and then all that had an end. We came to Canada. We spent 13 days on the ocean. Stormy days and sunny days.

Sister Coelestine, 1928: We went on the steamer, towards evening. And we were on the steamer singing all the songs we could remember; by the next day already I was seasick. The North Sea is quite rough. And then we saw those seals: they were just close and sitting there on the rock. And we kept going. It was getting rougher and rougher every day and at six days we had a tornado, and we had fog. I should mention, we had to take a small steamer up, and far to the north, to Greenland. The ship was going to Canada to pick up wheat. It took 13 days on the ocean. Sister Rhabana, she wasn't seasick, she always took a little drink, I was wondering how she kept it up, and one day she gave me a little drink, too.

Unidentified Voices: At the beginning it was fun, but at the end we got sick, all of us. Except maybe two. We were so sick. When we left the ship I thought, I'll never go back. It was quite strong a wind. I think, practically all of us were sick.

We left in January '36, and we were in the first quota of '36. We had to leave by quota. We wanted to leave in '35, but the quota number was reached. So in '36, we were one of the first groups to leave Germany in a very stormy winter voyage across the Atlantic. We were supposed to cross in 7 days from Wednesday to Wednesday, but it took 9 days because of the storm. And the sailors who were on ship, in all their experience on the ocean, they had never witnessed a storm like this. Of course we never knew how terrible it was because we never had any previous experiences. And it was very hard, and I was seasick for 7 days.

We sang in the evening when the sun was setting, and we sang with the Jewish women in four rounds, and it was really beautiful. The wind was so strong, and Sister got so sick and somebody ran and got the doctor. She had no pulse anymore, so I said, I throw all my relics in the ocean, and I tried to open the windows. We had relics with us, and the very moment I threw mine out the storm stopped. Sister recovered immediately.

Mother Bonaventura's Diary, 1925

A choir sang *Nun ade du mein lieb Heimatland* – Good-bye now, My Dear Homeland! What emotions overcame us with these wistful parting melodies! Our tears welled up upon sight of the great water. *Columbus*, the magnificent ship, was already waiting for us. It was the evening of the 29ᵗʰ day in July, the feast day of Holy Martha and Mary Magdalena, when we embarked. All guests were allowed to tour the ship, which really resembled a glorious palace. It was nobly appointed, as if made for a king or prince.

First, the table seating had to be assigned and the cabins chosen. Then we toured together with our Reverend Mother and His Excellency, the Monsignor, the first and second-class rooms when we already heard the command for the guests to leave the ship. A quick good-bye to Mother Aquinata and Father Schaefer on the gangway and ... it was achieved – the parting from our fatherland.

Presently, we climbed down to our cabins totally devoid of air and light, and then hurried back up on deck to wave a last farewell after the departing train and our loved ones.

We were exhausted and retired to bed, but couldn't find any sleep. Those narrow beds! There was quite a commotion when the upper bed had to be mounted by means of a ladder!

In the morning at 5 o'clock, Sister Gallena woke us up, "The ship is going to depart!" That we wanted to see. Within a few minutes we stood at the railing and watched with the greatest interest how this colossus of a ship started to move. We had to wait for the tide to go out in order for that to happen. The small pilot vessel would guide the giant ship into the open sea.

The captain took his post on the command bridge, and - close to us at the railing - a young officer called his commands down to the men on the dock by way of a mouthpiece. On command, they untied the thick ropes only to tie them up again on iron posts a few meters down. Slowly, very slowly, the ship started moving.

Then we were called to Holy Mass. A very emotional moment! A German Father, on the way back to the land of his mission, read Mass. Besides us sisters, some world travelers and a dignified elderly priest of 82 years received Holy Communion.

The piano in the ladies' parlor was made into our emergency altar, complete with the necessary wine and bread.

During Mass, we sang German songs. Especially *Geleite durch die Wellen* – Guided Through the Waves - had never been sung with as much conviction.

Another father read a small daily Mass in the 3rd class smokers' parlor, and our sisters served.

The ship's rocking motion started to become uncomfortable. We felt seasick and had to catch fresh air on deck.

After Holy Mass, Father made a short speech that began with the following words, "In nomine Domini! In the name of the Lord we begin our journey and hope for and ask from God a happy crossing!" Each day, the dear Father delighted us with another edifying speech.

After the second Holy Mass ended, the *Columbus* was already traveling the seas - free and proud. What a sight! The rising waters, and nothing more than sky and water. We never felt God's greatness and almightiness as manifest as at sea. Seagulls accompanied us for a whole day, a peaceful-solemn sight.

The bell called us for first breakfast. About 800 fellow passengers joined us in 2nd class, twelve priests among them. Besides their homeland, they had visited the Holy Father in Rome on the occasion of the anniversary of the Center of Christianity.

In company of so many priest and sisters and good people, we did not feel lonely or strange. Bishop Bahlmann resided in 1st class. When reading Mass, Reverend Professor Dr. Heidingsfelder von Eichstädt, who traveled to America to visit a friend, assisted him. The professor was a faithful friend to us throughout our trip. Also, the bishop visited us every day.

We spent our free time on deck exclusively, walking around, watching the cascades of water displaced by the ship, or resting on deck chairs, praying, and writing letters. Gradually we got to know the other passengers, especially the children. We received daily letters from the dear motherhouse. That was always good for some hullabaloo! Even the other passengers got interested. Packages with useful or amusing trifles were unpacked. Our good and thoughtful Mother had written a letter and filled a travel basket for every day, but only I knew that. So, every time, it was a joyful surprise that served its purpose: to keep away our homesickness.

The Reverend Bishop had recitation for us on three occasions in the cabin of the Franciscan sisters. We were happy. The dear Lord was so good to us.

On the first night, the *SS Württemberg* passed us; she was on her way home. Both ships signaled greetings, and we sent our greetings along.

On the second day, we anchored in a channel outside the French harbor Cherbourg. Passengers came and went. What commotion in the water: all the boats and sailors! The same again on the third day, outside the English harbor Southampton, whose green hills greeted us so friendlily. Warships crossed the waters; there was a fort very near us. After a two-hour stopover, the *Columbus* started moving again; and the next morning we were on the Atlantic Ocean. We couldn't get enough of the green waters with their peacefully rising waves. Quietly, the steamship glided along; in the distance we saw other ships passing.

On August 4th, we celebrated the feast of our Holy Father Dominicus. Heavens had provided us with a glorious day. We were allowed to attend the mass of His Excellency, the Bishop, and in the afternoon rejoiced in a fine lecture of His Excellency. On this day, the *Columbus* was a floating little convent of the Holy Father Dominicus.

On Sunday morning, 10 o'clock, Bishop Bahlmann read the Holy Mass with a sermon in one of the 2nd class dining rooms. All believers joined in when the beautiful Old German hymns *Hier liegt vor deiner Majestät* – There Lies Before Your Majesty – *Maria zu lieben* – Mary to Love – and *Wunderschön Prächtige* –

Beautiful Glorious - were sung. A floating house of the Lord.
Very deeply moving!

We were at sea for one week already; she lay so quiet and
majestically beautiful. For long hours, we looked into the green
depths. And once in a while – to everyone's great enjoyment –
fish shot out of the water high into the air, only to disappear again
into the sea. Long since, passengers hadn't been strangers to each
other any more. We had also found good friends for whom it
was a pleasure to give the same friendship to us, for example to
buy beverrages, because the heat as well as the thirst was great.
May the Lord bless and protect all these good people! Much ado
prevailed everywhere. When we wished to see the innards of the
ship, a steward was kind enough to show us around: engine house,
galley, 1st and 3rd class, the life boats and how to handle them, the
green house, the large smoke stacks, and more. The largest
smoke stack had such a dimension that a freight train could easily
pass through!

But as grand as the sea journey was, bit by bit we started to
look forward to the new continent, to America, our destination, to
our new homeland.

Thursday evening, August 6th. "Tomorrow morning we will be
entering port!" Such goings-on everywhere on board! Before
dawn, everyone was packed and crates and suitcases loaded on
deck. "Land, land," it sounded everywhere. There, in the pre-
dawn, appeared the green woods of the North American
continent.

We greet you, new Homeland!

Ships and boats of all kind began to criss-cross the waters, and
from one of those the physicians on duty boarded our ship. In
long processions we passed by the doctors to receive our clean bill
of health. At about 10 o'clock in the morning, the *Columbus* was
anchored outside of Brooklyn port. Then we all stormed the

otherwise inaccessible command bridge. What a wonderful view to be had from there!

A boat came to collect the mail, which the *Columbus* had brought from Europe. Letters and packages tumbled through a long hose – similar to the ones used by fire brigades – down to the boat. Then our ship was set into motion again, only to enter the port of Brooklyn after a short time. Standing at the railing, we tried to spot our dear Sister Belina, who had already traveled ahead of us on May 16th.

The hour arrived in the afternoon of August 7th, around 4 o'clock, when we were allowed to leave the ship after inspection of our papers by the appropriate officials and a second examination by the physicians. At the personal request of His Excellency, Bishop Carroll, the *Bureau of Immigration of the National Catholic Welfare* had sent a lady onto the ship to escort us to the *Leo House*, a hospice run by the Catholic diocese, where we would stay until the afternoon of Sunday, the 4th.

Sister Virginia stayed with her brother, Mr. Mathieu; Sister Mitis and Sister Gisela with her uncle, Mr. German; Sister Eugenia and Sister Walburgis with her relatives, the Weber family, and we others stayed at the *Leo House*. Saturday morning, a German *Fräulein* guided us to the hospital of the Reverend Dominicans in Brooklyn. How joyously surprised were we when the good sisters greeted us in German und offered their hospitality. We even encountered sisters from the Palatinate homeland. Brooklyn is a German settlement. The first sisters arrived there in 1853 from Regensburg on the Danube River. Mother Augustine won us over in a heartbeat. We only regretted to have to part so soon from this homey place. We only saw very little of New York, this great big city of the world.

Arrival in America

Mother Bonaventura's Travels

The following memories of Sister Birgitta and others remind us of the fact that Mother Bonaventura ventured back and forth, to and from Germany almost annually, to accompany the new sisters that had been appointed to go abroad.

Sister Birgitta, 1928: We landed in Montreal and then went to Chicago. In Chicago, Mother Bonaventura turned us over to the car, the driver, to bring us to the convent. We knew a little English, but not much. So the driver was a colored man, asking us questions, and all of it in native English. It sounded different to our ears than from the way we had learned it. And the first thing was -- we did not know where we were going. He could have driven us any place -- we wouldn't have known. Then he finally delivered us to a colony of German-speaking sisters, which was in the poorer section of Chicago, where we stayed three days, tired of adventure and being alone. We didn't see very much of Chicago: we only went along the street blocks and visited some stores but did not buy anything.

From Chicago we went to live in Milwaukee. In Milwaukee we had a nice drive. We saw Milwaukee for two, three days, and then we went on the train for our last trip to Helena. First, the train ride was endless. We were not used to such long train rides. In one way it was nice, in one way it was boring to us. We were in the open prairie, and the train stopped, and we were told by the train conductor we would reach Helena earlier if we would move to the train on the other track. We preferred to do that instead of going all day long. They took all our bags and baggage and stuff on the fields, in order to catch the other train.

We reached Helena in the morning of September 29th; we were three weeks on the road. At 8 o'clock in the morning, they were all surprised to see us because they didn't expect us until the evening at 8 o'clock. We had to take a taxi to get there, and then I remember, when we came, Sister Gisela was standing there with her apron full of decorations for the house where two of us sisters lived. And when she saw us coming out of the taxi she dropped everything. She was so astonished to see us. Well, the house wasn't decorated but we were glad to be home.

Sister Marina, 1928: When we came to New York, there were only two sisters that had relatives in New York. They took one sister, and Mother Benigna took another, and the rest of us had to stay in a boarding house for a day and a night. It was a big hotel but very old. During the night when we turned off the light, we scratched and scratched and scratched, and we turned the light on, and the bed bugs were crawling all over us on the wall and in our shoes. We said, is that our punishment going to America? Finally one sister was so badly bitten she went out of the room and the next morning complained to the clerk. And the next night we were put in another quarter, and at least we could sleep a little bit.

The day after, we traveled. It was all arranged by the railroad agent. We could not speak the language, only one sister, and we were transported on the railroad, and we were on our trip to Helena, and it took us two to three days on the train. The eastern part was nice: green fields, and as soon as we came more west, it was more like a prairie. We didn't see any trees, any people, any farms for miles and miles, no birds flying, no animals, nothing, only wild horses. Oh, we almost cried, we were so lonesome, and when we came closer to Helena the Bishop sent some assisting ladies to meet us before Helena, and with flowers to welcome us.

Later we came to Helena and were escorted to the college, and our first sight was the college chapel, and we had a benediction and a blessing from the priest. The only thing we could sing, we were so happy, was in German. We couldn't sing in English. Then after that, we came down to meet the Fathers; all the Fathers were standing around and outside.

Sister Coelestine, 1928: Montana. We didn't know what was coming next. We were just waiting for, you know, for the nice country. Outside, it was all prairie. We'd never seen anything like that at all. Oh, it was all right. We thought, the good parts are coming yet, but I was looking for something nice that kept you up good. Then we got going, we were on the train already two days, and we came to Helena in the morning. It must be quite early, seven in the morning I think. There was not a soul around at the depot in Helena. So, now we started out, the 8th of September, and we came there the 29th of September. I was sick most of the time. I had hardly eaten anything. But anyway, Mother Bonaventura was going up and down the depot and finally she found two taxis. Sisters were expected to come pick us up, you know, naturally. Oh, everybody was happy, they expected us in the evening, and suddenly we came in the morning. So we went over to the dining room to get something to eat, and Sister Hermetus brought something right away, they were here since 1925, and we came 1928. So they were a little worked in. She brought dry cereal, and I had never seen anything like that. I couldn't eat it. So, that way it went.

Sister Gerlanda, 1933: It took us four days on the train and, finally, when we came to Helena, oh, it was so nice. We could see how the country is, and we saw a cow out there, or a horse. We just shouted because we liked everything so much. And here came Father Riley, and he was the first priest I met in this country, so he was very nice and talked English, but I could not understand one word. Sister Padraig was in the library. She was young, and I was young, and we had a lot of fun there and laughed always when we couldn't talk. So we had nice time. Then we went to Conrad from there to see the sisters, and from Conrad we went to Shelby, and from Shelby we went all the way through the mountains and to the amusement park. We sang all the way and, really, that was so nice, and that conductor on the last day, he gave us a nice breakfast, and he never heard so many songs, and he loved them.

Sister Padraig, 1928: It looked like I was getting off the last station in the world. All these barren hills. Helena is quite a distance from the mountains and it did look barren, but I really got to love it in a year or so.

Mother Bonaventura's Diary, 1925

On Sunday afternoon, August 9th, a representative of *Catholic Welfare* took us to the New Jersey train station. His Excellency, the Bishop, had bought our train tickets, and they had to be extended four times because of the long waiting period.

Now we would proceed with the dreaded train travel by land. We rented a living room compartment, so at least we could eat our meals in private. For sleeping purposes there was room for four sisters; the others slept in second-class compartments.

It was great fun every night and morning, when the Negro man came to make the beds and help the sisters with climbing up and down, respectively. We had the greatest interests for the sights of the New World and we were eager to let nothing escape our attention. Only too soon the shadows of the night enveloped us and veiled the romantic waterfalls of the new world. Sleep came easily, against all expectations.

The next morning found us on a wide plain filled with forests
– which, however, rank well below the well-groomed German
forests – and farms.   I had forever been interested in the
American farms; I could never really imagine them.   Now we
were here, and I could see them with my own eyes.   Throughout
the train ride, farmers were busy to bring in the grain harvest –
August 10th! We are never that late in Palatinate.

In the evening, we reached Chicago and, after one hour,
continued to St. Paul where we had to wait for three hours the
next morning. In the lunchroom of the station, we twelve foreign
travelers caught the attention of a Catholic travel group.   After
Sister Belina told them about the point of origin of our travel and
our destination, a gentleman donated 10 dollars for our breakfast
and different ladies bestowed on us four boxes of candy.   God
bless forever those friendly people!

In a fruit and vegetable store nearby we provided ourselves
with some fruit for the voyage.   At 10 o'clock, we boarded anew
the train of the "Northern Pacific" only to – finally – disembark
again in Helena.   On this last day of travel, our tired limbs gained
back their elasticity in anticipation of our close destination.   We
had informed Bishop Carroll by telegram from St. Paul of our
impending arrival.

In Bozeman [Montana] we received a telegram with the
following content:

Helena, Montana, August 12, 1925
Reverend Sister Bonaventura
Care northern Pacific Number Three Livingston, Montana
Committee of Ladies will meet you at Station in Helena.
                                                            Bishop Carroll.

The closer we came to the much longed-for goal, the more
our hearts began beating faster, not only in delight, but also in
trembling uncertainty of all of the things expecting us in a different

country, with different people, a different language and different customs. But how could we be anxious after having experienced so often the extraordinary guidance of the Divine providence? In East Helena, His Excellency, Monsignor V. Day embarked on the train to greet us and to receive us in the name of His Excellency, the Bishop.

Arrival in Helena. On August 12, at 7 o'clock in the evening, we arrived in Helena. His Excellency, F. Heithoff, Brother Kelley, Brother E. Curley, Brother Z. Sherrin and some ladies had come to greet us, take care of our hand luggage and take us in their cars to the college. After greeting some reverend professors, our first visit was with our Divine Savior in the tabernacle of the college chapel. Him, we begged to bless our beginnings. For Him alone we had come.

His Excellency, the General Vicar, led us there and asked us to sing the "Te Deum". Not much song wanted to rise from our uneasy hearts but we had to thank our good Lord for so much, and because of that we tried for a vigorous "Almighty God, We Praise You". Monsignor himself was moved. Afterwards, our destination was the convent, our future home. It is a real little monastery in structure and furnishings. We felt at home immediately. Our luggage had already arrived before us. After some sustenance in the large dining hall of the college and sending the following telegram to Speyer, "Greetings from Helena from your sisters", we began to settle down in the convent.

First, it was necessary to shake off the dust and soot that we had brought with us from the long ride through America, and not only on our feet. The magnificent bathing facilities in the house had never been so welcome as on that evening. The veils were in need of new bows. It became midnight before everything was done and we could think of sleep. But those American beds! Those thin little pillows in contrast to our wide and thick feather pillows. Instead of the featherbed we only had two blankets.

That was something! To make matters worse, it was very severely cold, and on the next morning every sister complained.

We rested until 8 o'clock. Father Kelley, our first chaplain, was gracious enough to read a small Mass for us in the chapel of the college at 9 o'clock, in honor of our Holy Father Dominicus. The good father did this for us on many future occasions and has proven himself to be a good, reliable friend to our sisters. We will be thankful to F. Kelley for that always.

First Visits. For the afternoon of August 13th, several visits had been planned. First and foremost, the first visit with His Excellency, the Most Reverend Bishop, had been set for 2 o'clock. Reverend Fr. Heithoff, F. Sherrin, and a student took us in their cars to the bishop's house. We waited for His Excellency in the parlor.

For the first time, I felt bitterly grievous for not speaking nor understanding the English language. The Lord Master came to welcome us. In laying his hand on her head, the high church dignitary blessed every single sister and welcomed us wholeheartedly. We all felt that we had found a father in His Excellency. Sister Belina delivered to the bishop greetings from His Excellency, the Most Reverend Dr. L. Sebastian in Speyer, and from our Reverend Mother Prioress. Bishop Carroll thanked us for coming. How pleased he was to finally be provided assistance for his college, which he said we should look on as our own.

In Reverend Fr. Heithoff, of German descent, the bishop gave us our first confessor.

The bishop appointed the time for the consecration of our chapel and the benediction of our house for August 15th, St. Mary's ascension. We chose the Holy St. Mary Magdalena as our patron saint.

From the Bishop's house we went to the *Good Shepherd* orphanage. Mother Mary of the Holy Cross and several sisters welcomed us already at the entrance with sincere affection. The pupils sang several songs in our honor and recited some pieces of music. Reverend Mother Superior led us through the different rooms. Such cleanliness and orderliness are beyond reproach! After a refreshing beverage we took our leave to meet with the reverend sisters at St. John's hospital. Here, also, the same affectionate welcome.

In St. Vincent, theological exercises were going on. On our way to the orphanage, we toured the magnificent dome. We especially liked the glorious windows from Munich. At the orphanage, again, we were greeted cordially. But we longed to go home again, because we were literally dead tired. The first seeds of friendship with the new homeland were planted.

We used Friday to straighten up and put away our clothes, linen, suitcases, etc.

August 15th, Feast of Mary's ascension: This holiday stood in the sign of the Lord's words, which he had once uttered to *Zacchaeus:* "Today, salvation was granted to this house." Already at 7 o'clock in the morning, His Excellency, the Bishop, proceeded with the consecration of the chapel and the benediction of our house, assisted by Reverend Fr. Curley and F. Kelley. Together with the priests we processed around the house. How arduous this walk was for the Reverend Bishop! Then, the Lord Master celebrated the first Holy Mass in our chapel and Jesus, our Lord and groom, took up residence in our middle. Since this memorable hour, our dear little chapel has become our home in a strange land. During Holy Mass, we sang German hymns. Afterwards, the bishop paid tribute to our singing by saying in German, "*Das* [sic] *Gesang war sehr schön.*"

The fine altar of the chapel was a gift of the very venerated mother of the college president, Dr. N. C. Hoff, Frau Hoff-Brennan. May the sisters of this house always demonstrate through their intercessional prayers their gratefulness to this noble benefactress and all her living and deceased family members: this noble lady and her family are especially included in the *Novene* before each Friday of the Heart of Jesus.

As at any occasion in America, a photographer was in place. A picture was taken in front of the west side of the house: His Excellency, the Bishop, in the middle, around him the sisters, and on both sides the assisting priests and attendants. It was bitterly cold this morning, and a boisterous storm made taking the picture almost impossible. How happy we are now to possess such a picture: *Reverend Bishop Carroll, Founder or the First Foundation amid the First Sisters.*

After His Excellency had breakfast, he came to the convent again to talk over some things and to inquire about the well being of us sisters. We talked about the dreadful cold that robbed us of our sleep. Over and over the bishop insisted that we look at the college as our own and proceed accordingly. In the afternoon, a delivery of comforters and throw rugs arrived. Thousand fold "thank you" to the dear bishop who is now resting in the Lord. The comforters have served their good purpose to no end and are a constant reminder of him.

In the afternoon we wanted to write letters, because "abroad" so many were longing for news from us. We had just started, when Reverend Sr. Hypatia, Superior of the S.V. Academy, arrived with another sister to show us the academy. The retreats were closed for the morning. The two sisters took us by car – of course – where everyone awaited us and treated us only with geniality and love. But how could we make each other understand? Oh dear! We didn't understand English, and the good sisters didn't understand German. That was sad and funny at the same time. Why only this language bedlam in the world? And yet, we conversed for some time. Sr. Belina was under some distress to translate it all. In the evening, the good sisters had an American dinner prepared for us. They and we did our best.

At 7 o'clock, Monsignor Day gave a slide presentation about his excursion to Italy. We were to stay and sing some German songs afterwards. We were only back home at 9 o'clock. Sr. Hypatia stayed our devoted friend. We will not forget this dear soul in our prayers.

Sunday, August 16ᵗʰ, finally, was filled with letter writing.

On August 17ᵗʰ, we began our service at the college with the commencement of the priest retreat for Bishop Carroll and about 70 priests. The residing cook took care of the kitchen, Sister Virginia, Eugenia and the postulant Hedwig assisted him. He was supposed to stay on until the sisters had mastered American cuisine. The other sisters attended to the rooms of the reverend professors and priests, served at meals and did the dishes.

We were used to hard work, and yet, in the afternoon, we each one were so tired that we were hardly able to walk anymore and had to rest for an hour to be able to be back at work in the evening. After four days, the first battle was won and the rest of the break – 14 days – were used to clean. There was plenty to do.

The sisters even washed windows up to the third floor, a really dangerous task in America. Bishop Carroll sent over Fr. Sherrin to advise us not to do that.

In the meantime, we could not befriend the American fish dishes. Even if German cuisine is not that versatile – and there really was not any abundance of food during the war and after – what we do have is meticulously prepared. This was indeed a sacrifice for each of us.

On September 1ˢᵗ, the Reverend Bishop laid off the cook and assigned all domestic chores to us. Sister Virginia was a trained cook with many years of experience, so she was appointed to the post by the Reverend Mother Prioress. Sister Virginia also had training as a baker: she had worked for three months in a confectionary. Sister Eugenia and Hedwig were also assigned to the kitchen. Sister Eugenia had also been working in a kitchen for many years, and Hedwig's parents owned a Club-Hotel in Düsseldorf, so she was well versed in cooking and serving.

In addition to the work assigned to her, Sister Arsenia was to study diligently the English language to enable her later – after a replacement arrived – to take over a school as soon as possible. Sister Walburgis officiated as the registrar and did the sewing and darning. Sister Belina had the difficult task of translating, in addition to her work. Sisters Gallena, Gisela, Jukunda, Klodia and Mitis were to tend to the professors' residences, classrooms, guest rooms, offices, halls, dining room, scullery and to serve at meals.

Although it was Reverend Mother Prioress' emphatic wish not to serve the students, it could not be avoided. Reverend Fr. J. O'Neill, Vice president of the college, said, "To preserve your own peace of mind, I want to ask you to take over the serving." It really did prove to be beneficial later on. Students don't have any business in the kitchen and therefore are not allowed in there (may that always remain so!). Always two sisters would be working together in the classrooms and residences of the reverend professors. In that way, one sister is the guardian angel of the other.

The Reverend Bishop had planned his departure for Rome for September 7th. We wanted to finalize a contract before that. The American law does not allow for a contract with people or institutions in a foreign country; it could only be concluded between the college and us sisters. Bishop Carroll had Mr. Walsch, attorney-at-law, execute the contract, and Reverend Fr. Hoff signed it.

Before leaving for his travels, His Excellency laid out the prayer blessings: we were supposed to handle everything in the fashion we were used to. It was also his wish that we'd attend High Mass on Sundays at the College chapel and sit in the first row on each side. Furthermore, he had a laundry put in so that we could take care of our own laundry.

We asked Mylord to also grace our motherhouse with his presence during his European travels, which he gladly promised to do. On September 6th, His Excellency came over to bid his farewell. "Will you be needing an more sisters?" asked the Bishop. This was a question after my own heart, for I had realized from the first day that our number was too small to get the work done, and I answered, "Oh yes, at least three."

"I believe there is room for five," the Bishop answered thereupon. Before his departure, the good Shepard blessed each single sister, again laying his sanctified hand on each head. We had only been acquainted for three weeks, but still this short time was sufficient enough for us to care for him from our hearts. His leaving was painful for us who were still suffering greatly from our own leaving. On the evening of September 7th, His Excellency departed from Helena.

On our arrival, only a few professors had been at the college. After 10 weeks of summer school they had been seeking some recuperation, even Reverend Dr. N. C. Hoff. One can appreciate that we awaited anxiously the return of the head of the household.

All the other professors had already returned, before we could finally welcome the president on Sunday, September 5th. Dr. Hoff is of German descent. How great was our joy, when the reverend president greeted us in German! There is no doubt that members of one nation feel naturally closer to each other. Nature had linked us together and, later on, many more demonstrations of friendship tied us even closer together, and with the greatest gratitude we will stay beholden to this good gentleman always. In spite of all of his work as professor and president, throughout two years, he painstakingly taught us the English language during one hour each week. May he be repaid with everything good for his faithful services. This experienced head of household knew advice for everything. All of us hold in high esteem this noble and pious priest who made so many sacrifices, and we count ourselves lucky that we were allowed to begin our service in America under his protectorate.

[There are no further entries in this notebook with the title, Early Days at Carroll College [the name later chosen for Mount St. Charles College], as recorded by Mother M. Bonaventura, 1925]

Mount St. Charles – Carroll College

The sisters never again saw their benefactor, Bishop Carroll. He arrived in Speyer on October 28, 1925, and he spent a few days at the Motherhouse. While on his way to Rome, he died on November 4, 1925, in Friburg, Switzerland.

The following history of the sisters is an account of the Chronicle of the Dominican Sisters of Immaculate Heart of Mary Province:

The times after Bishop Carroll's death brought many hardships. And the sisters had expected hardships, realizing that no work of God prospers unless it is watered by tears, fortified by sacrifices, and accompanied by insults and misunderstandings. There were certain priests among the college faculty to whom the mere presence of German sisters was an annoyance. They tried their best to make life miserable for the sisters so that they finally would give up and leave the college.

For several months, the sisters labored in a surrounding that mistrusted and ridiculed them. Small wonder that they were contemplating to leave the college and look for a house in the city of Helena where they would support themselves by needlework. To Germany they would never go: they did not want to heap such a humiliation upon their Motherhouse. Thus, in prayer and in tears, and by patiently waiting for God to dissipate the clouds, the time arrived when the two priests who had labored painstakingly for the removal of the sisters left the place on their own accord. One of them had the grace to ask the pardon of the sisters before his departure.

One obstacle was smoothed out, but poverty clung perniciously to the sisters' path. Not the poverty they were obliged to practice by their vows, but the poverty that compels one to go without the barest necessities. The college was highly in debt and could not afford to pay a big salary to the sisters. Mother Bonaventura was frequently ill.

Upon one occasion there was no money in the house to buy some medicine for her. Two sisters, while cleaning Father Kelly's room, told the good priest of their dire want. He pulled out his purse and asked them to take the offered sum. Many a time, there were not even three cents in the house to mail an important letter. We, of a later generation, pay high tribute to our pioneer sisters. Their endurance in sufferings, their prayers and tears have straightened out the road for us, who followed. Their wants have enriched us; their perseverance inspired us. May God bless them abundantly!

There are few spoken accounts of this time.

Sister Coelestine, 1928: We had a lot of boys there. We had 150 boys. We washed dishes. We took care of the Fathers there.

Sister Marina, 1928: We had no wash facilities at all. Our house was just finished before we came to the convent, and we had to send our first laundry out to the *Good Shepherd* and we could not because we had no money left, and the college was so poor, and those of us that taught could not get paid because we were so poor and everything was not finished. (Her voice sounds like she's crying.) And after a few weeks, some Irish Fathers did not like us German sisters. Some sisters decided that we go back to Germany, and I said no, I will never go back to Germany. I stay here. Even if I have to enter another convent. They sent us all alone, without any money.

Mother Bonaventura was our superior, and she got a very bad cold, and we hadn't even the money to pay for the medicine, so Sister Jucunda and I went over to the Father – we took care of his room – and he gave $5, so we could buy some medicine for Mother. Finally, after a year or so, Mount St. Charles got another president, and he was more compassionate with us, and he gave us more help. Some of the students helped us in the kitchen to wash the dishes. All of us young sisters had to wash the dishes and serve. Later on it got better, we got some help.

Sister Mitis wrote in her memories of her years at Carrol Mount St. Charles College: We wore large colored aprons instead of habits while performing the heavy chores of cleaning walls, doors, furniture, stairways, and windows of St. Charles Hall during the summer months. Everything was shining when we were finished. Mother Bonaventura and Sister Virginia provided snacks and refreshments, and here and there we stretched our legs and rested for a while. The job took almost six weeks. When the work was done we celebrated by parading around the kitchen and the large college dining room, carrying mops, rags, buckets, brooms, etc. and singing away.

We sisters took our meals in the sisters' dining room, a few feet down the hall from the kitchen. Sister Virginia ate lunch in the kitchen. One day, as we were eating lunch in the dining room, Sister Virginia appeared in the doorframe. Tears fell from her eyes and she dried them with the corner of her kitchen apron. Her weeping was caused by a sense of shame and humiliation. A while ago, believing herself alone in the kitchen, she ate off a large meat platter, using a heavy serving spoon, gobbling up the noon meal, when Bishop Finnegan entered the kitchen. He nodded and told her it was all right. But Sister ran out of the kitchen to tell us about the incident. We consoled her and asked her to laugh about the situation.

SOUTH SIDE SEEN FROM THE WATER TOWER.

Helena, Montana, early 1900

The First Hospitals

In December 1926, Monsignor Day drew Mother Bonaventura's attention to the old hospital in Conrad, Montana: St. Mary's. The hospital, founded in 1907, had changed management several times over the years and was in neglected condition. After many negotiations, the sisters took it over. Mother Belina was appointed superior. The other pioneers were Sisters Garina, Jucunda, Humilia, Lanfrieda, Marina and Loyola. Mother Bonaventura accompanied her little flock to the new place and stayed there for four weeks. Besides nursing the sick, everyone scrubbed walls, ceilings and stairways in all of their spare minutes.

A typical daily schedule for the tightly structured life of the sisters looked like this:

5:45	rising
6:05	morning prayers
6:30	meditation
7:00	communion
7:30	breakfast
8:15	Holy Mass
9:00	community work
12:00	lunch, recreation

1:00	community work
5:00	Compline
5:25	Matins and Lauds
6:00	supper
6:30	Rosary, night prayers, Salve
7:00	spiritual reading
7:15	recreation
8:30	Silence
9:00	Profound Silence
10:00	lights out

When there was extraordinary work that needed to be done, recreation and spiritual reading were replaced by taking on the tasks at hand, even during Silence and Profound Silence hours.

Many occurrences in the hospital illustrate its difficult beginnings. There was hardly any furniture in the sisters' quarters. The house chapel was not set up. The sisters chanted their prayers in the kitchen. One evening, they were saying their night prayers kneeling on apple boxes and improvised footstools. While they were thus engaged, Bishop Finnegan of Helena arrived. He came to the kitchen and, standing in the doorframe, took in the touching picture.

On some other day, they bought with hard earned little money their first few pounds of apples. Mother Bonaventura peeled them carefully for applesauce. When it was ready to be served at the table, the cook discovered to her great dismay that salt instead of sugar had been used for the precious apples. And how they had looked forward to their first applesauce!

Yet, St. Mary's Hospital prospered, and the number of patients soon proved to be too large for the small place. Plans were drawn up for a larger building.

The successful operation of St. Mary's Hospital prompted the sisters to lend a willing ear to the proposal by Father J. Stang of erecting a new hospital in his parish, in Chewelah, Washington.

On July 12, 1929, Mother M. Bonaventura wrote a letter to His Excellency, The Most Reverend Charles D. White, Bishop of Spokane, in regard to the new venture.

> The writer, Sister Superior of the Dominican Sisters in charge of the domestic department of Mount St. Charles College, Helena, Montana, begs to introduce herself to our Lordship. In August 1925, we came to the United States at the call of the late Bishop Carroll. On the first of January, 1929, we started a small Hospital in Conrad, Montana, which belongs to the diocese of Helena. We sisters now number twenty in this country.
>
> Complying with the request of Rev. Joseph Stang, Chewelah, to send sisters for hospital work in his parish, I have asked permission from our Venerable Mother Prioress, which I received by cable. We are anxious to accept this invitation as soon as we can get more sisters from Germany. At the outset, therefore, I ask your Lordship's permission for the undertaking in Your diocese.

Bishop White welcomed the Poor School Sisters to his diocese, and their association proved to be a long and fruitful one. That's how twenty young German women of about twenty years of age, with very little knowledge of English, came to live amongst the miners, loggers and Native Americans of the Pacific Northwest.

The Pacific "Wild" West

A description of Chewelah in the early 20th century comes from the publication by Elizabeth Riley, *Still Strong Beats the Heart:*

There was a start of a business district with a hotel, saloon, dry goods store, post office and butcher shop. Joe Ray wast he first butcher. He would slaughter a small beef in the business part of the city. What was left went to the coyotes, and the bears took any other leftovers after sundown. When the village grew a little, folks began keeping cows. One could look up or down Main Street or the alleys and see cows being milked, morning and evening. Every businessman had a shovel to scrape chips off the sidewalk. Hogs were also kept downtown on a lot with plenty of mud for a wallow. Lee Kelly, who kept the Emblem Saloon, had a bear chained up to a large post, about 15 feet high. The bear would climb to the top of the post and watch the goings on below.

Mother Bonaventura recalls her coming to Chewelah: When we arrived in Chewelah, Father sent over beds for us, also a table and some chairs. We spent our first night here – all by ourselves.

Tomorrow is the big cleaning day. Men and women of the town will take part.

Sister Richildis, 1933: Mother brought us in the night and we didn't see so much. She did that on purpose (laugh). It was a farm, and we expected a big city. The cows were all asleep, so no mooing. In the night we had little visitors. The mice came and chewed on the cookies that we had left there on the side of our beds. We did not have any bedside table. We did not have any closet. We had only our bed. We took two apple boxes together and put our wash pans on top and put our shoes under. We had no chair, nothing was there. The clothes were hanging on the pipes.

Sister Francis deSales, 1933: We went west, to Washington, and we lived at that time on a farm about a mile out of Chewelah. Mother thought it was not civilized, so we went at dark, along the dirt roads. We were sent to go to bed and it was so poor, there was nothing there. Just a big hall and no divisions, no table, the only things were in our trunk. We hung our habits onto the wall. We really cried because it was very great poverty. We were not used to this.

The next morning, Sister said she would show us around. And I thought the town was nearby. It was quite a walk. We put on our clothes and she laughed. She had her sleeves rolled up and I wondered about walks in America and she said, put your old clothes on because we are going out in the country. So, as we walked, we saw a pasture and eight horses and I remember I neighed like a horse and the horses answered me. Then, they ran away. When they came around again, we screamed and ran. The male horses came close and a dog rushed up and stopped the horses. It made me so worried, I never did it anymore. It was our first outing.

Farming in Chewelah: St. Mary of the Pines

Mother Bonaventura had been considering buying a large farm, formerly owned by the Benedictine Sisters of Clyde. It was located near Chewelah on the edge of a beautiful forest, and it seemed an ideal place for a convent and a novitiate.

Mother Bonaventura saw the place for the first time on May 22, 1929, and wrote to Bishop White, "The farm is offered to us under the following terms: Time-payment: $ 4,000 yearly for 20 years; or Cash-payment: 50,000..."

Reverend Joseph Stang strongly supported Mother Bonaventura's enthusiasm for purchasing the farm.

March 25, 1931 was the big day of the dedication of the farm St. Mary of the Pines. Mother Bonaventura describes it as follows for her sisters in Helena, who could not be present:

> His Excellency, Bishop Charles D. White of Spokane, arrived on the evening of March 24th. He asked to see the chapel and liked it very much. I had audience for an hour. On March 25th, at 9.30 o'clock, a procession was formed, which started at the hospital and proceeded towards the farm. The bells of the parish church were chiming and it... rained! The bishop rode in Mr. Rulzer's car. Everyone said it was a beautiful procession. I myself did not see it. I was in the second car. Besides the bishop, five Jesuits were our guests: Reverend Vice-Provincial W. Fitzgerald, Rev. F. Tomkins, Rev. George Weibel, Rev. P. Joyce, Rev. C. F. Owens. After the blessing of the chapel, his Excellency said Holy Mass. We sang *Tota Pulchra; Wo in feierlicher Stille; Magnificat*. Sister Carina played the organ. Father Fitzgerald preached the sermon. The religious life was his subject. Many Catholics from town attended the ceremonies. Our

chapel looked like a jewelry box. Mr. Thomas took
several pictures. I shall send you some as soon as they
are ready. At 1 o'clock the bishop blessed the
Novitiate and the Stations of the Cross. Then, the
priests took their departure.

Mother Bonaventura was now in charge of two houses – St.
Joseph's hospital and the farm St. Mary's of the Pines. A diary
was lying on the hospital desk. Some of the notes Mother and
Sister M. Jucunda jotted down in the years 1931-1934 read as
follows:

1931

March 25: Dedication of the farm
March 26: Sisters Eugenia, Ludolfa, Loretana and
     Reginalda are living at St. Mary of the Pines.
March 31: The Novitiate started.
April 14: Prominent visitors at the Hospital and at St.
     Mary of the Pines: The Right Reverend, Bishop
     Finnegan of Helena, and the Rt. Rev. Bishop
     White of Spokane.
April 17: Sister Marina taken ill.
April 20: Mother Bonaventura and Sister Belina left for
     Oakland, Calif. to attend the meeting of
     American College of Surgeons.
May 2: Mother and Sister Belina returned from their
     trip to California.
June 11: Father Eitel, chaplain of St. Mary of the Pines,
     arrived at the convent.
June 29: Sister Marina still ill, left Chewelah today. She
     will stay for some months in Helena to gain
     back her health.
July 10: Father Rebmann, S.J., arrived at St. Mary of the
     Pines to spend there some quiet days.

July 14: Mother's Feast day. Sisters from the hospital at St. Mary of the Pines to celebrate. Father C. Thuente, O.P., arrived to spend his vacation at the convent.

August 2: Miss C. Hatfield guest of the convent.

August 4 Feast of St. Dominic. Final Vows of Sisters Rhabana and Coelestine, First Profession of Sister Erwina.

August 5: Sister M. Erwina assigned to St. Joseph's Hospital.

August 15: Final Vows of Sister Loyola.

Sept. 4: Sister Aquilina transferred to Helena, Mont.

Sept. 14: Sister Gallena appointed to take Sister Aquilina's place in the laundry.

1932

Jan. 23: Mother Bonaventura and Miss Mary Ghekiere from Williams, Montana arrived today at the hospital. Miss Ghekiere will be our first postulant.

April 14: Bank of Chewelah closed up today. Some people were hurt pretty bad. We had only $ 2.43 there.

July 10: First Profession of Sister M. Reginalda. Reception of Miss Ghekiere, now Sister M. Dominica.

Aug. 1 Everybody went picking cherries: Mother, Sisters Arsenia, Gallena, Jucunda, Lanfrieda, Marina, Loyola, Loretana, Milburga, Ludolfa, Reginalda, Erwina and Dominica. Sisters went via school bus to Kettle Falls.

Aug. 14: Sad news arrived from Helena, Montana. Bishop George J. Finnegan died suddenly.

Aug. 15: Mother left for Helena to attend funeral services of Bishop Finnegan.

Sept. 23: Mr. Bauer is not faithful. I (Mother) told him to look for work elsewhere. Will he go? We must reduce our workers, because we're unable to pay wages.

No further notes in Mother Bonaventura's desk diaries of 1932, and none of 1933, can be found. The years at the farm are redolent with bitter hardships. Mr. Bauer proved to be insincere and unreliable. The few sisters worked beyond their strength. There was never a balance between the money invested into the farm and the income from the farm products. Prices sank lower and lower. One must recall that all over the country it was the time of Depression. Finally, the sisters were compelled to look square into the face of the situation, realizing that running a farm had proved to be a failure and that the only way out was to sell the place.

The following letters explain the proceedings from the time when giving up the farm was contemplated, to the time when the community took over an old mission in Ward, near Colville, Washington.

Mother Bonaventura to Mother Dolorosa, Superior of the Convent of Perpetual Adoration in Clyde:

St. Mary of the Pines, Aug. 7, 1933, "As long as the prices for farm products are so low, the farm will never pay itself. Since we are here, the price for cream never went higher than 25c, most of the time it is only 18 or 19c. You know all about the other prices for wheat and stock.

It is impossible to defray the taxes, wages, repairs and so on by the farm income. I found out that we made a great mistake in taking over the crop of 1930 and the machinery. At the time we bought them, the prices were still high; soon after New Year of 1931, they dropped and dropped. The machines are so worn out that for the money we paid for repairing, we could have gotten new machines. But all is according to God's Holy will and we must be satisfied."

Mother M Bonaventura to Bishop White:

St. Mary of the Pines, Jan. 17, 1934, "The Dominican Sisters of Chewelah, Washington, submit to Your Excellency the following petitions:

1.   As we personally explained to Your Excellency, because of the troubles we meet here on the farm, the many difficulties, chiefly resulting from the financial depression and the bad farm conditions at present, and because the debt of about $51,000 is too great a burden upon our small Community, we humbly beg Your Excellency to grant us permission to negotiate with the Benedictine Sisters of Clyde, and to cancel the contract regarding the property of St. Mary of the Pines.

2.   In case that it should become necessary that we must give up this farm at Chewelah while Your Excellency has gone, it may also be necessary for us to look for a place to which our novitiate is to be transferred.
We humbly ask Your Excellency to grant permission for a temporary transfer of the Novitiate to another suitable place, which we believe to have

found in the Colville Sisters' Mission. The Jesuit Fathers to whom the property now belongs offered us 110 acres and the building at the price of $5,000, payable with 5% interest. The buildings have not been in use for several years, and repairs must be made, estimated at $3,000 maximum. We are humbly asking the permission of Your Excellency to acquire this property. May we also be allowed to have at that place a chapel, in which daily Mass can be said and the Blessed Sacrament be kept? We will be careful that everything is arranged according to the prescription of the Laws of the Church. And may the priest who will attend to the spiritual needs of the Sisters, have the necessary faculties from Your Excellency?

At the same time we heartily beg the Episcopal blessing of Your Excellency for this new enterprise.

Mother Bonaventura to Mother Dolorosa:

St. Mary of the Pines; Jan. 25, 1934: "... In our preceding correspondence we informed you always about our difficulties and hardships on the farm. In 1930, when we drew up the contract, everything looked promising, and with courage, even enthusiasm, we started, but soon became aware of the mistake we made in burdening upon ourselves the large property. We were told that the farm at least would pay itself.

We were not at all afraid to work and to meet our engagements.

But disappointment followed after disappointment. In this short space of time we sacrificed much, invested much money into the farm, not seeing any result.

Certainly, you were always well acquainted with the prices of the farm product: how they went lower and lower, and how deplorable farm conditions became. So it happened that we even invested more money from our missions into the farm than we made in the same time here on the place.

His Excellency, our Rt. Rev. Charles D. White, Bishop of Spokane, is making his ad minina visit this year. Before His Excellency left for Rome, we submitted to him the farm problem in its difficulties. His Excellency gave us permission to negotiate with you in order to cancel the contract. This is the only way for us to come out of the debts, which our small community is not able to carry and to pay.

Bishop White to Mother M. Bonaventura:

Spokane, Wash., April 4, 1934, I am pleased to give my approval to the project, as outlined in your letter of March 31, to purchase the Jesuit property near Colville to which property it is your intention to move from your present location at St. Mary of the Pines. I earnestly pray that the proposed transaction and your new home near Colville will be found satisfactory to you and your community. May Our Lord bless your undertaking and guide your community in the way of His Holy Will. I enclose a small personal check. I wish it were much larger.

St. Mary of the Pines, Chewelah

Out in the Potato Fields

Our Lady of the Valley Convent, Kettle Falls

S o it was decided to move the Motherhouse farther up the Colville Valley to Ward, Washington. Just opposite the historic Jesuit Mission of St. Regis, about seven miles west of Colville and not far from Meyers Falls (today: Kettle Falls), was the large building formerly occupied by the Sisters of Providence, who had come to the valley in 1873. Here they taught white girls and Indian girls in the Sacred Heart Academy until 1921, when dwindling school enrollment caused them to leave the academy.

Thirteen years elapsed before the Dominican sisters discovered Sacred Heart Academy and decided that it would be the ideal locality for young girls to receive training in the way of Dominican life. Nestling among the mountains, its picturesque location appealed to the sisters and, on April 25, 1934, the community took possession of it. God's promise of an abundant life came true at this place in the Colville Valley. The setting - a broad green valley with a mountain backdrop - offered nature in all its richness. The new motherhouse became an independent Province, and Reverend Mother M. Bonaventura was named Mother Provincial.

However, the abandoned buildings needed much repair. Eventually, the old place would be transformed into an ideal setting for convent life, but at the beginning, the sisters report about many hardships:

Unidentified Voices: The night we came, all I could see was dark; it was midnight. I thought, gee, that looks small. I couldn't figure out how we'd have enough room in that place. We couldn't see that it goes on in the back. There was one sister, we had to stop three times, she got so sick. When we came from Spokane, we were with Mother Bonaventura. It was just as dark as it could be and she kept saying, "Children! Look out! Look how beautiful!" (laugh) And she said, " There is the crucifix that is lit up, that is going to be your home from now on." And when we came in the dormitory she said, "Isn't this a beautiful place? You all sleep in here, it's so beautiful."

Green curtains! I was so thrilled to be at the convent because I could have curtains around my bed. In Speyer it was all open. And the terrible noise in here! It was the pack rats. Terrible. We always had something in back running and I said, "What is that?" Some rats up there. Oh my God! That noise was terrible!

Sister Benigna, 1937: We worked hard. But it was a pleasure. I don't know. It was just, everything. Oh, the wonderful thing was, when we came to Kettle Falls and we came there at midnight. They had great big tables full of cakes and coffee and we really celebrated that Advent in Kettle Falls.

The nicest thing I remember was when we came up to the dorm. Now you would call it kind of crude, but there we had green curtains. And we thought we were in heaven because in Speyer it was just an open dorm. We had no privacy whatsoever, and as poor as it was in Kettle Falls, we thought we were in heaven because we had those green curtains and we had some privacy. Because I was brought up at home rather bashful. And in Speyer you had to undress and get dressed in front of everybody. It was terrible for me, and I think for the rest of them, too. You almost closed your eyes getting dressed and undressed there.

We hardly had any furniture, just a rough table that was made later on. I don't think we had anything. On each floor there was a washroom with several sinks and showers. That was all, and we had our German bedding for a time.

That water was so terrible out there. Oh, and we used to collect rainwater to wash our hair. We worked a lot. We worked and prayed. We had much joy to work.

Sister Mary Magdalene, 1937: We had hardly any water. We had water until 11 o'clock at night. We fetched it and Sister said we were late. "I can't even depend on you." And we fetched more water until it was time for prayer. The mission took the water in the daytime and in the nighttime we had little pressure, very little. That's why we had to fetch water in the night, to keep things growing. Sister Hedwig came and said they had watered this and that place and it was my turn and Sister Alexander's to keep watering. We had to track the hoses down and hang them up again because we didn't have that many hoses. And run all the time to the river. At the river there was a pump. It was for the dishwasher at the kitchen and I had to turn that off at 8:00 p.m., when I got off.

Sister Mary Esther, 1937: I remember picking potatoes by the river. We'd have to go down every night, late, and turn the pump off. Usually Sister Michael was there. One night we came back late and had a good time, we talked and we sat at the edge of the bathtub and washed our feet. When we got caught, we got a scolding.

Unidentified Voices: We had running water for the bathrooms, but it was just for the bathrooms: for the washing opportunity. So in summer, on August 9th, when the heat went on for a long time, the water shortage became critical and we had not enough for the bathrooms. It was a problem, so we filled buckets and carried them throughout the place, and it was critical we had to save water, taking showers instead of a bath. It was critical for that time, all summer. And we also hauled in water from tanks from Kettle Falls, at times. It would supply us for a few days. And later, when Arsinia came in, she saw it and said, "This is our most urgent problem, to provide water." She asked Carroll College at that time if they had any money to extend our water supply, and they laid the pipes on the other side beyond the hill, and it proved to be a very good move because it gave us plenty of water.

When we took over *Our Lady of the Valley* convent, it was run down. It had been empty for 16 years but the building was still standing. There were no locks, no doors and the first night, they settled in the place that later became the laundry room. They couldn't lock the door so they packed some furniture in front of the door, so they felt a little bit secure.

We saw that quite a bit had been done to the place, to make it livable. They had fixed up the plumbing, so hot and cold water was there, and in the kitchen there was the dishwashing equipment, and there still was a woodstove and a box you had to fill all day long. Outside there was a good pile. Father Phillip made it a point to cut our wood, to fill it for the kitchen. And we gathered in the kitchen very often when it was cold. Outside, when we came, there was snow lying. We came on the 10th of February, 1936 and the snow covered the place around. The lawn had been planned but not yet planted. The holes went down for the trees. As soon as it thawed, we planted the trees and little by little put the lawn in.

Single rooms were not many made yet. I think, just for Mother Superior, Mother Seraphia, they had those single rooms, in the first hall above the chapel. And for the rest of all of us, we slept in the dorm. And the dorm had been open for all of us, and we put curtains around that they had brought from St. Mary of the Pines. Also the bed linens. That was nice, all the things they had brought along from there.

Days took on shape, and everyday life developed.

Sister Benigna, 1937: In Kettle Falls we had, oh, we had great times there. We'd get mad at each other, but we worked and we had practically to hand-water everything in the garden. Sister Alexander, she was just a tiny little nun. She had a big vegetable garden. And that whole lot, where the apple trees are, we dug over ourselves. There was nothing but roots and leaves, and so we dug over that whole big lot by hand, you know, with spades, but you didn't mind because it was fun. It was such a challenge.

And the laundry, it took us practically all week to do the laundry. But then Sister Bengalis was in charge of making butter and Sister Mary Anne baked bread practically every other day because we ate so much. Our appetites were ravenous. I gained 30 pounds that year, really! I weighed 136 lbs. after the Novitiate. We had fresh bread and the good butter. And we had apples and we worked hard.

There was a lot of ironing. We had these corslins and forehead things and, ah, we just had that little bitty mangle that you had to crank by hand. They were long hours, but we really enjoyed it. And we went on marches, you know, we had a flag in front, and they told us, we don't do this in this country. We walked on the open highway and sang German songs and had the flag from Kettle Falls. I wouldn't have wanted to miss those years.

Sister Catherine, 1933: We walked two and two in the garden and sang. We had special songs. I really enjoyed it. There was a long storm in 1935. We made a bonfire and Brother Philip was mopping the chapel. We walked in, and the first ones up front carried a banner. It was a sign of our unity. We sang songs and Father blessed us, and all this time we had Novitiate.

"Come on, let's all get together at the end of the day and have a refreshing drink." We had all good appetites. We really enjoyed it. We were very close. Father Phillip used to call us the "eleven *Kinder*" and he taught us English.   He used to be teaching. And in those years, we were in different schools.

There was absolutely nothing at the convent, except four walls and a floor, and our sister made cupboards. We tried to get this all done before the other twenty-one came. There was nothing but green curtains. We had no money to buy anything and we put the shelves up. So when they came, there was an absolute sense of freedom, not having to watch what you're saying, what you do. First the wideness of the country, the immensity. Then we went out there singing. We had so much fun.

Unidentified Voices: I stayed. I was the only girl in five years, and I took care of the chickens, the milk. I made butter and that's when I first learned the American songs, when I first would memorize it. *My country 'Tis of Thee,* and all those verses. *Old black June,* and all that. I never heard them sung but Father had given each one of us a golden songbook. Father Philip was so good to us. He was in the motherhouse when we came and he had a nervous breakdown. He gave us English lessons, but we couldn't ask questions because he was too nervous to answer them. If we ever asked a question, we would write it down. And he wrote notes all the time. Oh, but he was a Holy man and we really respected and loved him. He did very much for us because he had come from Germany and he knew the things that would be hardest for us and he gave us many pointers of language and how to understand the country and all.

And then there was Mrs. Hatfield, the Dominican beneficiary. We loved her. She had a little dog, a little bit of sunshine, and she carried him around all the time, but we got lessons from her and we just loved that she was good to us, too. She taught us many things. I remember one time, we all had ribbons in our hair and she said to us, "You dress up. You have good appearance and you feel happy," and she said to think of the many who would have to go out and do all these other things, thinking that would bring them happiness but it wouldn't.   I remember that so well.

The spirits of the high school-age postulants from Germany were high. Sister Consuelo especially remembers the singing.

Sister Consuelo, 1937:   We came to this country like a cyclone.   We were 16, 17, 19, and we were full of life, full of songs, full of ideas.   We were intelligent, we were enterprising.   We marched through Kettle Falls singing and carrying a banner, singing German songs. Father Phillips said, "Children, you can't do that, they will think you are German spies.   People don't march through towns and sing."

It was a terrible privation to not be able to march through Kettle Falls and sing, so we marched through the garden with our flag, and one day Father Phillip gave us money and said we could march to Marcus, which doesn't exist anymore.   "You can walk there and come back by bus. I give you the bus fare, and I give you a little money for drinking something."   And we seven of us drank something at Marcus.   We took a bus and it was a great undertaking.   And the Holy Spirit must really have been there because we really prayed.

I think I prayed more then than I do now, although I may pray more genuinely now.   And we gave each other conferences there.   We talked to each other there about everything.   We were very close and we were forever watering plants, watering trees and paths, and we were forever in the laundry scrubbing those hard hems of those habits.   And we were mangling and ironing and singing, and singing, and singing.

Phillip liked us very much.   He bought us things all the time.   Each one got a dictionary.   And I remember one Valentine's Day, he gave us a whole jar of honey and on it, it said, "Honey for my Honeys."   He always had something. Benigna had to make his peanut butter sandwiches every single night.   And when I came to

Helena in '42, I saw peanut butter and I said to Sister Rhabana, "Do you think I could have some peanut butter?" And she said, "You can have all the peanut butter you want." It was the first time that I tasted it.

Sister Marianne made the bread. They had fresh bread and I was always hungry, but I lost 20 pounds just in the first year. It was just the difference. I put on 30 later. And we were always hungry, so when they were at prayer, we went and got a whole loaf of fresh bread and she got us the butter and we had apples and we ate that whole loaf of bread and fresh butter. We were seven of us. And I remember, Mother Bonaventura always said, "You eat us out of house and home."

And how we ran up and down the steps and, oh, how she scolded us. And we talked German and she printed all over the place "Speak English Only", over the whole place. (laugh). Then we started doing that for 5 minutes and then buh-huh, buh-huh. Remember when the doorbell rang and we all disappeared and nobody wanted to answer it?

One thing that we did in Kettle Falls, I'm sure someone must have mentioned it, how much we walked, how we took a sandwich and walked and walked through fences and under fences: our pleasures, our recreation, was utterly simple.

And we were given nothing. We were given very, very little understanding by those sisters who came here originally, who did not know what had happened in Germany since they left. We had grown up in the Hitler times, and although we were not his followers we were influenced by the spirit of the time and we found no understanding for our youth or our problems or for our solitude. They really didn't even know how to make use of our talents properly. But then I'm not judging them either, because they could only do what was in their capacity, but we really didn't fit into the framework to which we came. There was much suffering, which was borne heroically and silently. No one made much of it.

Improvements were speedily made. The sisters' industry and persistence transformed the building, and soon a home for the hired help (the *Men's House*) was constructed, and *St. Thomas Hall*, which served as a gymnasium and contained rooms for classes in art and printing.

Before long, velvety green lawns and graveled walks surrounded the buildings, and a riot of colorful flowerbeds. Close to the river, a vegetable garden was planted. The well-groomed grounds offered great opportunities for summer-time picnics. A summerhouse was built and, in the main building, the kitchen and dining room doors led directly outside. All of this and the grotto of *Our Lady of Lourdes* would lead the observer to suppose that the place had been cultivated for years.

Construction became almost perpetual: dormitories, a meeting hall, a more functional kitchen, a library, a bigger chapel, and more – to make room for the growth of the community and the hundreds of guests who would come for retreats throughout the years. With a sunken garden, grotto and preening peacocks, the convent grounds became a place of inspiration.

A flourishing farm was at the back of the convent and a herd of Jersey cows grazed in a green pasture. The fertile land yielded apples, apricots, cherries, strawberries, raspberries, corn, peas, beans, tomatoes and other produce. Chicken clucked happily in the chicken house. Near it was a pigpen.

The animals and the garden required hard work, but they provided the sisters with eggs, milk, meat, vegetables and fruit. There were sausages to make, hams to cure, cows to milk, canning, cooking and, as Sister Birgitta recalls, "the constant picking of raspberries from June to September." Much of the credit for this successful farm is due to Mr. James Drew, who was overseer and manager of the farm work for five years, first at *St. Mary of the Pines* and, since the move, at *Our Lady of the Valley.*

It took his continual care and hard work to improve the farm and make it pay.

The sisters' hard work also included cleaning, sewing, and the never-ending laundry. To a community whose dress was a white habit, laundry took a high priority.

The old place was transformed into an ideal setting for convent life. During the summer months, sisters from the Dominican hospitals and schools traveled to *Our Lady of the Valley.* They arrived for rest, relaxation, and for the annual retreats, spiritual exercises in which the sisters in silence and in prayer renew the inner resources, which give strength, joy and courage to carry on life's daily struggles. Later on, the *Lady of the Valley* convent served as a laywomen retreat house.

A journal from the archives tells: Our first retreat is over. A group picture was taken, even though it rained; a chicken dinner was served and the ladies were very happy and satisfied. Everything went smoothly. We sisters were tired, but happy at the success of our first retreat. Sister Theodula handled the cooking and food preparing very well. We had 16 retreatants – more than we expected. We gave Father Joseph Grady, S.J. a check, which he handed back to us, saying, "From the Jesuit retreat house for the start of the Dominican retreat house."

The sisters from the Colville and Chewelah hospitals sent us help. Sister Gisela washed dishes, Sisters Mary Agnes and Donatilla served at the tables. As they were leaving, the sisters from Colville took along the bad linen and Sister Marina in Chewelah washed the table linens. All had helped us willingly and cheerfully.

The Newsletter of Kettle Falls reports about one of the little incidents that makes life interesting:

Oh Sister! What was I supposed to do? I was so embarrassed. I almost died.

But, Sister Mary Thomas, what on earth happened?

What do you mean, what happened?   I tell you what happened: I poured the gravy down her back, that's what happened.

You did what? Down her back? How?

"Well, there was Sister Gertrudis, and there I was with two dishes of gravy. I just sort of leaned over the table to put one of them down, and while I was leaning, the gravy in the other dish was pouring down her back. I didn't even notice it.

Well, what did you do then, for heaven's sake?

Oh, I didn't know what to do. I just stood there and watched it slither down her veil onto the floor. Then I gently tapped her on the shoulder and whispered that there was a little gravy on her veil. If only Sister had been a Franciscan, the gravy hardly would have shown. Oh, well. (Sigh) It came out, almost. I guess some people get all the gravy.

In *A Measure of Leaven* – a documentation about the German sisters' history in the American Northwest – the Kettle Falls convent and provincialate is described as the center of Dominican life: As the Dominican's expansion era leveled in the late 1940s, life took on a pattern, and *Our Lady of the Valley* was the center of it.

As headquarters of a large, complex enterprise, the provincialate teemed with activity. The teaching sisters spent summers and retreats there, and those who worked at hospitals came regularly for retreats. Christmas celebrations, feast days, picnics by the summerhouse, badminton on the lawn, and plays they wrote and performed in their gym punctuated the more serious pursuits of prayer and worship, work and service that filled the sisters' days. Departures and homecomings were frequent, as sisters moved from assignment to assignment, returned to visit families in Germany, went away for study, and attended professional conferences.

What began as a handful of sisters, cooking and cleaning for a men's college, had grown to a community of 32 sisters at the end of 1934. But, as much as they had already accomplished, the greatest challenges still lay before them.

The Kettle Falls around 1937.
The falls are now below the Lake Roosevelt Reservoir.

OUR LADY OF THE VALLEY CONVENT
MOTHERHOUSE AND NOVITIATE
1934-1970

Our Lady of the Valley Convent in Winter

Retreat in the Lovely Gardens

Colonnade at the Convent

In the Chapel

Every Day was Laundry Day

Walking the Countryside

St. Mary's Mission, Omak

In July 1935, his Excellency, the Most Reverend Charles D. White, summoned Mother Bonaventura to his office to ask her if her community would take over the Indian Mission in Omak. Mother wrote to her motherhouse in Speyer, Germany, to inform Mother General Aquinata, O.P., about the request.

The history of the Indian Mission in Omak is most interesting, as documented below by Mother Bonaventura in her journal about St. Mary's, 1941. The mission was established as St. Mary's Mission in 1886 by Father Etienne de Rougé, a Jesuit, and the first priest ordained in Montana by Bishop Blondell.

Mother Bonaventura's Diary

Father Etienne de Rougé

The indefatigable push of the Catholic missions to win the Red Man to the Church is vividly shown forth in the devoted service of Rev. Etienne de Rougé on behalf of the Indians of Washington State. Father de Rougé was one of the best known and most successful priests who ever entered on a life of toil among the Indians of the Northwest. For the conversion of a neglected people, Etienne de Rougé renounced honors in his

native land – France – came to America in 1881, and founded in
the State of Washington a mission that has since developed into a
place of learning and civilization, which has spread its beneficial
influence throughout the Colville Indian Reservation and far
beyond.

It was shortly after his ordination that Father de Rougé
instituted St. Mary's Mission in the Okanogan Valley, below
Tonasket, Washington, which now stands as a splendid
monument in his memory as a pioneer Indian missionary. In
1888, other buildings were added through the help of kind
friends, particularly Mother Katharine Drexel. The crude log
cabin, which Father de Rougé built as a nucleus, still stands a half-
mile from the present mission at Omak. Elegant proof of the
success of the work was the group of mission buildings erected,
including church, rectory, convents, school buildings,
entertainment hall, gymnasium and various farm buildings.

The natural virtues of the Colville tribe Indians are honesty,
bravery, love of truth and fidelity to wife and children. These
virtues, the pagan Indian believed, would earn for him future
happiness in the happy hunting grounds. The opposite vices, he
believed, would bring him everlasting suffering. In this tribe,
these natural virtues have been strengthened by fidelity to the
Church and to the Christian duties.

Wherever we have proof of spiritual progress among our
Okanogans, we can without difficulty trace the Catholicity back to
the mission school. Therefore we can safely say that all spiritual
progress is chiefly made among the children who have attended
Catholic schools. It is they who keep up the pious customs of
former years, camping near the church during great festivals,
taking part in our processions and receiving the sacraments with
regularity and fervor.

In their great variety and various forms, the Indian languages
are as much a mystery as the origin of the people. The Indians

have never used a written language. The grammars now in use / existence [sic.], are the work of fervent missionaries.

What the Mission School Means

Mother Bonaventura's diary continues to describe thee influence of St. Mary's Mission to the Okanogan tribes.

In the early days of St. Mary's Mission, Chief Nraamelt of the Wenatchee tribe came to the missionary, Father de Rougé, and asked him to come to his people. When St. Mary's school at Omak was started, the pioneer Father de Rougé gathered all the children of the camp. The Indians wanted a Catholic school. Some parents passed the winter at the mission so as to keep the children in school. The priest was to teach them.

Father de Rougé wished to erect a Catholic school, but no one wanted to help. If discouragement had triumphed over him he might have abandoned his seemingly hopeless task. When he would speak of a school the answer would be, "It is impossible." When he would ask for help, the answer would be, "We have already too much to support."

Often the priest had not even sufficient clothing. Once, going to Yakima, he had to borrow the hat of an Indian and put on an old pair of boots left long ago at Chelan by Father Grassi, and he could have put his two feet in one of them. Yet, the school started.

After a while, with the help of the Indians, the priest built a schoolhouse. An old Indian did the cooking and helped to preserve order. After an enforced absence from the mission, Father de Rougé was overjoyed to come back and find the school going on the same as if he had been home. That good Indian had installed himself as watchman over the children and saw that all were at school and behaving well out of school hours.

Thanks to the mission garden and orchard, the children were provided with food. Two Christian Brothers then came to teach school. Father de Rougé sought for ladies who could and would help him. At last, in 1907, he secured the services of a lady teacher living near Tonasket, a Madame La Londe. A few other devoted women joined her in the work and they formed themselves into a society, calling themselves Lady Missionaries. They assumed a simple black habit and followed the exercises of the religious life as close as possible under the saintly missionary's direction.

The following ladies lived and died there: Medames La Londe, Clark, Blake, Luce, Desmont, Fitzgibbon, and Kemper. Careful instructions were given to the boys in many branches, such as farming, printing, carpentering, masonry and gardening. St. Mary's at this time boasted a museum, a brass band and a baseball team.

Conditions at St. Mary's today are very different from those of a quarter of a century and longer ago. Under the influence of the Catholic religion, the adult Indians have progressed and encourage us with hopes for the future of the tribe. The children are docile and fervent. On church feasts, especially on Corpus Christi, Easter and Christmas, the Colville Indians gather from near and far. Numerous tipis and camp fires in the Indian village in front of St. Mary's Mission, and about five hundred Indians representing the various tribes of the Colville Reservation, coming on horses, in wagons, in automobiles: that is the scene on the eve of Corpus Christi.

The Indians spend that day in approaching the Sacrament of Penance and in beautifying the mission grounds and Indian cemetery with decorations. Dawn on Corpus Christi brings many visitors from the neighboring towns. The entire congregation takes part in the procession. The canopy over the Blessed Sacrament is carried by four Indian Chiefs. Thus the Divine Master is brought in procession to bless His children's land and to receive His children's homage. Benediction is given at two improvised altars. The chiefs speak, urging their Indians to love their faith.

Occasionally, Confirmation is administered to one of the school children and to a large number of bronzed and wrinkled Indians. Holy Communion is brought to the sick and the aged who cannot leave the shelter of their tents. Truly, the Master comforts the afflicted and blesses all, as He did in His Sacred humanity. He walked the earth.

Father de Rougé died May 9, 1916, having labored for thirty-one years among the Indians in this part of the Northwest. Rev. Celestine Caldi succeeded him at the Mission and watched over the spiritual welfare of the Ladies. In 1939, four of these Ladies remained. They were: Mesdames Riedmiller, Foster, Carroll and Jacob.

At this time, Father Caldi applied to the Dominican Sisters at Kettle Falls for help. They were then unable to give it; but at the request of the Bishop, our sisters assumed control of the Mission, July 1, 1936. The Lady Missionaries entered the *Convent of Our Lady of the Valley* in the Order of St. Dominic. The school for Indian boys and girls opened the first week in September with Mother Seraphica in charge, Sister Francis de Sales teacher for 5th, 6th, 7th and 8th grade, Sister Aristelle teaching 1st grade, Sister Richildis music teacher, Sister Donates for home economics, Sister Reginalda for cook, Sister Marina for laundry and housework.

The buildings of the mission at this time comprised sisters' convent and apartments, two dormitories, classrooms, two playrooms, kitchen, chapel, gymnasium, auditorium, a rectory, farm buildings and a large church.

Three years ago, July 30th, a terrible fire started in the kitchen, consuming the main part of St. Mary's Mission. It took only two hours to bury so many valuable, unselfish sacrifices of the heroic missionaries.

God's ways are inconceivable, and He in his goodness turned bad into good. The extensive gymnasium soon was remodeled into a proper apartment house, comprising a suitable kitchen, the dining rooms for fathers and sisters and children, a parlor, two classrooms, a playroom for girls, a music and a sewing room, a laundry in the first floor, a beautiful chapel, an infirmary and the apartments for the sisters in the second floor.

The children are a great means of bringing their parents to God and to the Church. They are coming from the different parts of the Reservation, staying here for nine months, enjoying the benefits of a Catholic education.

The keynote of St. Mary's Mission is cheerfulness. Visitors of all creeds assert that the time spent here is most happy. We work, we toil, we fell and saw trees. We clear the fields, we beautify the landscape in front of the houses, we take care of the garden, we seed, prune and irrigate. We are poor, but God is blessing our work in the spiritual progress of the children and their good influence over their parents.

St. Mary's Mission July 26, 1941

Father de Rougé's Nuclear Log Cabin

Native American Family

History

There are many misunderstandings about mission schools. Most people know that Indian children were often taken away from their parents to be forced into schools and stripped of their Indian customs and language. But those schools were government-regulated schools, not mission schools, and government agents took the children, not missionaries.

Carlisle School was such a school that had opened its doors to the Indian youth of various tribes and its agents made propaganda trips to the West. The children of Indian parents often were taken without the free consent of their parents. The government agents knew how to intimidate the people and how to make attractive promises. Quite a few children from the Colville Reservation attended school either at Carlisle, at Chemewa, or at Fort Spokane. To the great sorrow of their parents, some of the children were never returned to them.

Mission schools, on the other hand, were not mandatory, and they respected the Indian customs and language of the children. The Okanogans had a language of their own – the Indian Okanogan dialect – and were very particular about being instructed in this language at St. Mary's. Father de Rougé and later Father Caldi spoke the Indian language very well and could teach successfully, while the Dominican sisters did not have this advantage. They were not understood by the homesick Indian children. The sisters at first had to teach them English word for word before they could give them any lessons at school. However, the sisters often didn't know English very well themselves. The sisters were mostly teaching the girls and it was very hard to acquaint them with another way of living. Their parents watched the white women taking care of the girls. If the fingernails were cut or if there were any deviations from their age-old customs, trouble followed.

It was a great privilege in pioneer territory to have a school for the children. Therefore, the families would gladly make the sacrifice and move nearer to the Mission during the school year.

- The children would go to Mass, then home for breakfast.
- 9:00 a.m. they came back to school.
- 11:30 a.m. they went home for dinner.
- 1:00 to 4:00 p.m. they were in school again.
- 4:00 p.m. they would say the Rosary at church and the night prayers, and then they were dismissed.

Later, boarding houses were built, and the children would only go home for vacations.

St. Mary's Mission was to take care of the various tribes of the Upper Columbia and Okanogan valleys. For many years, the mission hospital was the only hospital available in the Okanogan county. Informants have mentioned the multiple cases of tuberculosis that existed especially among the Indians and partly among the Whites during the early 1900's and later. Tubercular children were sitting in the classrooms among the healthy and were sleeping in the common dormitory. There were absolutely no means of isolating the cases, and even the little hospital in existence was ever too small to meet the needs, in spite of several additions. It is understandable that a great percentage of tubercular people could be found at the Mission, hoping to receive help.

The Mission educators had a very positive image of the American Natives.

"Intelligent by gift of God, respectful through tradition, the Indian is very religious in character. From time immemorial, he has believed in God, the Creator and calls Him "He who has made." They pray, singing: "My Creator, I do not know where you are, but I pray to you." (de Rougé)

"The Indians say grace before meals, knowing that it is God who gives the food. They still go and pray on the mountaintops to be near "Him who made." They would fast several days in order to obtain a favor, even that of becoming a sorcerer." (de Rougé)

There was a certain magnanimity and nobility of heart in the Indians not found too often among Whites. An example of this was Mrs. Matilda Wapato, the mother of Dr. Paschal Sherman [St. Mary's Mission's name today is: Paschal Sherman School. sic], one of Father de Rougé's honor students.

Mrs. Wapato was called to attend the murder trial of her husband's nephew who had shot Mrs. Wapato's husband in the year of 1905. A dispute about family property had caused the attack. Mrs. Matilda Wapato made a sudden end of the murder trial, yet her grief must have been profound: Suddenly she stepped down from the witness chair and faced the jurymen ... with tears coursing down her cheeks, she spoke and gestured eloquently. *"Me man dead. He go setting sun. He go up there. Hang him by neck,"* and she pointed at Ignatius, the nephew, who was on trial, *"make him die. Would this second die bring back my boys' father? Hang him by neck you accurse him before God. Me no like that. Me no like my family defiled before God. No good. Me witness no more.*

There were many complaints about the loose living, the bad example of some Whites and how they took advantage of the Indians. Among them were whiskey peddlers, cattle rustlers, horse thieves, gamblers and others.

Antoine, chief of the Colvilles, stood up in council and told the government representatives: "We want you to take our part: the liquor is coming up to our knees; we tie our people up for drinking, but the whites do not tie or punish their people for selling liquor to Indians. I wish you, who come from Washington, would take our part and stop this selling liquor to us."

The last chief to give a talk was Weeh-ah-pe-Kun or Kis-a-wee-likh, sub chief of the Okanogans. His speech was especially touching, for it tells us how the incoming whites were undermining the authority of the chief and of the Indian parents. They were degrading the moral life of the Indians generally, that had been on a high level among the aboriginal Okanogans:

"When the Whites come to our camp, the first thing they do is to steal our wives and daughters, and when I tell them to go away, and ask my wife and daughters to stay with me, the Whites abuse, threaten, and take my daughter to prostitute to their passions. When I follow their example and do the same to my fellow Indian, I get into trouble, I get my head broken, and punished by my chiefs. You don't punish the White man for the same conduct I am guilty of; I get punished for doing what they taught me. You tell us to stop drinking and not get drunk; the White Man makes and gives us whiskey, and then takes our women from us; the Indians are poor and ignorant but they don't deserve such treatment from the Whites. If they want to better our condition, let them stop bringing Whiskey in our country."

The town of Okanogan has been at all times the place where whiskey is sold to the Indians. There were held meetings, races and other events, where the chief object was to sell whiskey to the Indians and make them drunk, then get all the money they have. All the towns voted dry, but Okanogan was the only one that kept the traffic, and had plenty of trouble.

It was very difficult for the Mission work.

"The fourth of July every year we do not know what to do, as it is the beginning of the vacation of our children, and the first thing is to see the parents take them to this town, the mothers as well as the fathers drunk, and the children, boys and girls, all mixed up in the crowd. We had terrible scandals of course ...

Gambling is organized in town for the Indians on the days of meetings, and races, and money put up to encourage them to gamble." (de Rougé)

The Mission educators could tell many sad tales of mental agony endured by children of parents who were habitually intoxicated. Observation of the two greatest problems of the Colville Reservation showed that the whiskey problem and the broken home problem were interrelated and that each broken home seemed in turn to create as many broken homes as there were children in the family. The Mission educators were working against forces that they were not able to control.

Many of the Indians, especially the chiefs, had before been great stock raisers with hundreds of cattle and horses. After they became uprooted from their tribal possessions and their individual holdings, they became in most instances poor. The white neighbor was allowed to buy enough acres to increase his profits, while the Indians became poorer as the years went by.

Indian Inspector James McLaughlin:

"What he is, the white man made him – for in the Indian of today there is very little trace of that high spirit and cheerful independence which marked the aborigines. ... The Indian has been made the object of speculative persecution by every white man who felt that he wanted what the Indian possessed."

It may not be said that the education offered by the Mission raised the standard of living of entire tribes, which now depended on the economic development of the community and state, but undoubtedly it did raise the standards of living of the individual Indian educated.

Encampments at the Mission

The Indian tribes would congregate at St. Mary's on high feast days: Christmas, Ash Wednesday, Holy Week and Easter,

Corpus Christi and the feast of St. Ignatius. They would come to the Mission by horseback or in rigs, some traveling three or four days, with full camp accoutrements. Then they would camp around the mission for a week or so. Upon arrival, every Indian would first come up the little hill on which the Mission was erected to greet the priest

The annual celebration of Corpus Christi was a real event. The Indians knew it as the "Flower-Feast" because of the profusion of flower decorations and the flowers strewn along the paths of the solemn procession on that occasion. Between 700 and 800 people would attend, and the services and processions were truly marvelous and impressive. Colorfully dressed Indians could be seen forming at the church and seriously stopping at the various stations along the trail, down along the creek.

The tribal chiefs, with the throng foregathered on the campus beneath Japanese lanterns, delivered their addresses in different Indian dialects: eloquent, some fierce and forceful in manner, always inspiring and moving in the sentiments and counsel, so warmly proceeding from the heart.

These chiefs had quite an organization where every little detail of the camping order was regulated.

Every tribe had its camping place. The poles for the tents were left at the Mission; it was a matter of minutes to erect an Indian village. Indian policemen were constantly on duty, day and night. Church policemen saw to it that no drunkards or medicine men entered. The chiefs would hold places of honor in the front row on the right side, while the women prayer leaders had the front row of the left side reserved. The ushers wore special ceremonial sashes and were proud of their duties. Offenders were brought before the chiefs, this becoming a regular court procedure. Special herders were named to watch the horses. At nine o'clock at night, the curfew bell gave the signal to go to rest, and no visiting in the other tents was allowed.

Indians and Whites, Christians and pagans filled the church of St. Mary's.   The Catholics received their Lord in Holy Communion during the early Mass; later High Mass was to be celebrated. The Indian policemen guided the processions and maintained proper order and reverence among the worshipers.

Throughout the Years

"You had to travel over 200 miles, crossing rivers, forests, mountains and seven miles trails winding in the back of steep mountains above the Columbia river between rock and pine trees. The Indians call it the Seven-Devils trail." (*Diary of St. Francis Regis Mission*, October 9, 1889)

"Provisions to take along from the closest neighboring mission, St. Francis Regis: 160 pounds of flour, 36 pounds of dry meat and a few dried salmon. Travel took about a week. Trips were hazardous as the waters were high and the roads bad." (*Diary of St. Francis Regis Mission*, Mss., OPA, May 13, 1870)

Often, missionaries had to cross the Kettle River on the ice, sometimes finding it necessary to spend hours freeing the two packhorses from a hole in the ice. They had a sack of flour, a pot of lard, and a pound of salt: the only item on the menu was pancakes.

Afterwards, the old Indian trails became the rough wagon roads. Overland transportation took place by means of the saddle horse, the team and wagon, the stagecoach, and, during the winter months, the bobsleigh.

In 1901, you could get to the Mission on Omak Creek by freight team from the Columbia River, and then you had to go along the shores of the Omak Lake. At that time, there was a road, which in the course of years has been washed into the lake.

From Davenport, it took three days to reach St. Mary's, for the transportation was difficult: railroad, open stage, and ferry.

It took forty-six hours by steamer from Wenatchee. During the winter, the crew had to break the ice with dynamite.

The entire region around the Mission was in its original wilderness, and trees and underbrush were everywhere. Besides the Mission buildings, there were many cabins with hand-hewn floors; also many tents were pitched on the place.

The Mission property then consisted of a little garden, a few chickens, two cows and three horses. In 1899, a church was built. There was no floor in the church then, only grass, around which the sides of the church were built. The children used the church as sleeping quarters, wrapping themselves in blankets. During 1901-1902, the institution grew into two different buildings. One, adjacent to the church, contained bedrooms, classrooms and parlor. The kitchen, dining room and assembly hall were on the first floor, and dormitories only for boys on the second floor, in another building that had to be reached by going over a backyard. The teachers then were Gade Riley and Father de Rougé.

Winters were very hard and very cold. All froze, and water had to be hauled in, which made a great deal of extra work. All the potatoes froze, and even the fields had to be plowed over and reseeded. That meant a poor first crop and not enough to keep the few cattle over the next winter.

Summers were hard because no iceboxes and freezers existed to preserve the food for the Mission. All had to be either dried or salted. During the winter of 1907, Father de Rougé wanted to make an icehouse. The boys had to haul the ice from Omak Lake and place it in one of the root cellars they had along the hill. It did not work; the ice melted down when spring came.

The children were always hungry. It can be imagined that when the number of pupils grew, it was hard to keep them all fed in spite of the garden and fields. Oftentimes, they had a diet of dried salt cod and plain boiled vegetables, no milk, no butter, little sugar and plain bread.

A small house, 30x18 feet, became the beginning of the school. This would be the start toward a regular boarding school. For that purpose, another two-room house was built, 100x26 feet, with a little house on one side for the laundry. The new addition would consist of two classrooms and a dormitory for the little boys, and it would take still another addition to accommodate everyone. Also, outside buildings and sheds were erected. Orchards, gardens and parks were laid out and planted, irrigated with water from the falls of Omak Creek, where the boys had built a dam to collect the water.

Since metal pipes were not available, or they were too costly in this part of the country, square wooden ones were constructed and laid all the way from the falls to the Mission for domestic purposes. It was many years before these flumes could be replaced by metal water pipes. Various irrigation ditches helped water the soil and served as a demonstration to future Indian farmers.

The boys also had to help prepare and store food for the long winter months. During harvest time all who were present at the mission had to help peeling apples, slice, dry, and pack them in sacks, which were stored under the stage in the old auditorium. Apples, potatoes, carrots, turnips, and other edibles had to be brought into the root cellars along the hill, below the boys' schoolhouse. The Mission had some of its own grain; it did not own at that time enough land to be completely self-supporting.

The boys helped in every way: Harry Van Coelen of Portland, Oregon, who attended St. Mary's school from 1905 to 1908, even had to bake the altar breads, and when the sisters arrived, he showed them how to do it. Harry Buber, later living in Puyallup, had to help the hired man milk the cows, of which there were about twenty-five.

During Harry Van Coelen's time, the order of the day at the boys' school was as follows:

6:00	up, no heat, as fast as possible into clothes
6:30	breakfast: mush, bread, fried potatoes, coffee, never fruit
7:30	to Church
8:30	to classroom
9:45	recess
12:00	dinner: boiled potatoes, meat, gravy, etc. The food was good.
12:00-1:00	free time
1:00-4:00	back to school, except on days for special projects
4:00-5:30	chores – kerosene lamps to be taken care of, about 50 of them. The boys had to saw logs, split them, and fill the wood boxes all over the place, except in the dormitories.
5:30-6:00	supper
6:00-8:30	study time

Then, Father would come to tell stories or, in later years, the boys would go to Father's office for that purpose. Father would pick the boys for the story characters. He always stopped when the story was most interesting and the boys looked forward to the continuation next evening.

Outside of classroom and recreation hours, all boys had something to do on the farm and indoors. An establishment as large as the Mission, with farming and stock raising operations, required a lot of hands to keep it going. On the whole, the boys accepted the work as a matter of course and rather cheerfully. Few of them paid tuition fees. Their labors had a twofold purpose: To teach them agriculture, stock raising and such crafts as running the establishment afforded, including carpentry, plumbing, etc. and, in the process, to produce beef, vegetable, and fruit for the school. At that time the school produced a considerable amount of its own food, since the surrounding country was sparsely settled and the transportation of supplies by steamer or wagon freight rather difficult and expensive.

Beside their ordinary school subjects, the girls were taught how to sew and mend, cook and bake, and darn stockings. They learned how to keep house, wash and iron, and plant a garden. Every Thursday and Sunday would be half-free days for walks and picnics. They were marched in strict ranks, the bigger girls having charge of smaller ones. The sisters felt their great responsibility in supervising about sixty children on an outing. All could swim like fish and would not come out of the water until they were exhausted.

The separation between the boys' school and the girls' school was complete. Each school had its own household and its own cook. The boys had to wash their dishes, each one at his place; dishwashing bowls were placed at the head of the dining table and passed along. The girls, likewise, did their dishes. The laundry was washed in the sisters' house and two or three boys had to help in washing the boys' clothes.

Higher education had been introduced at the Mission school. Besides the elementary subjects, Latin, Greek, higher mathematics, bookkeeping, typewriting, music and art were taught. Brother Celestine, an expert taxidermist, started a museum. All kinds of rare animals and birds were on display. St. Mary's Mission's famous brass band had eleven pieces. Fine arts and sciences had found their home at St. Mary's. The Mission had the first high school and the first junior college in this part of Eastern Washington.

When the grounds were finally perfected, they were well laid out and took on a park-like appearance with beautiful lawns, flowerbeds, and full-grown shade trees. The buildings comprised the main boys' buildings, the convent and girls' school with laundry, the new church in a pretty park, a modern hospital with operating room, new gymnasium, band stand, an old building used mainly for employee quarters and storage, barns and field houses.

The bell of the new church was a piece of history of St. Mary's Mission. It had been shipped from Milwaukee to Omak in 1890, and had served the first house chapel. Through the decades the bell had pealed for the glamorous gatherings of the tribes in the Omak Creek Valley; it had given the signals for their religious and social gatherings. Every phase of the daily order from morning until night was regulated by this bell. It also served to announce the end of the earthly sojourn of many good old Indian people and accompanied them by its tolling to their final resting place.

The Poor School Sisters at St. Mary's

When the Poor School Sisters took over St. Mary's Mission, enrollment had shrunk due to the lowering of the educational standards under Father de Rougé's successor, Father Celestine Caldi, S.J.

In his reports on St. Mary's Mission in the *Omak Chronicle*, Mr. F. A. De Vos writes:

Father Caldi was as keen a chap as Father de Rougé, but he began his time under sad handicaps. He had no personal funds, no estate to help him and he came to Omak to ask me how a man who did not know a growing turnip from a potato vine could feed 140 youngsters from what looked like a good farm. He admitted he knew a pig was not a cow but what care to give them and how to use them were beyond him and he had to make the place carry all expenses. The solution was easy however. Tell no one of your farming ignorance, turn the farm over to Mr. Smith, the girls to the sisters and handle the boys' school and administration yourself.

The very next school year after Father de Rougé's death, the high school subjects were dropped. While standard subjects before included English, French, history (bible, American, modern and ancient), geography, arithmetic, algebra, trigonometry, Latin, Greek, music (piano, strings and brass), art (drawing and oil painting), bookkeeping, penmanship, science, physics, carpentry, elocution (including drama), under Father Caldi simpler courses in English and arithmetic with a good working knowledge of typewriting, painting, mechanical drawing, hygiene and physics were taught, together with some carpenter-, blacksmith- and dairy work for the boys and cooking, sewing, laundry and nursing for the girls.

With the decline of the scholarship came the decline of the school. Also, the beautiful gardens and parks had become cattle pastures; pigs were penned against the big school building to facilitate their feeding. Much of the land was fenced in; about 200 acres were planted in grain and some acreage in alfalfa. The orchard and some gardens were cultivated to furnish the vegetables. While during Father de Rougé's time, education was the number one factor and all other aspects of the Mission life were geared to this objective, now work became the important business of the Mission.

However, even if the educational standards of the Mission under Father Caldi were lowered, the children attending the Mission still received a far better training than they could have had at home.

Father Caldi was a builder. Especially after the great fire on October 15, 1919, when all of Father de Rougé's famous school went up in flames – including the museum, the library and all the great historical treasures of those pioneer days – Father Caldi knew no rest until a third, more fireproof set of buildings at the Mission were completed: the ones still in use at the Mission today.

While all the building projects went on, more and more classes were suspended. The number of qualified teachers decreased, and no new ones were hired. In about 1933, Father Caldi became aware of serious consequences if not enough helpers could be secured to care for the children. After he had been turned down by the Ursulines, the Providence Sisters and other sisters, he found out that a small community of Dominican sisters had just established themselves in their new Provincial House of *Our Lady of the Valley*. It was then that a letter from Father Caldi was received at the convent:

Ven. Mother Bonaventura
Meyers Falls, Washington

Rev. Mother:

You probably have heard of St. Mary's Mission and school. Our average enrollment is about eighty Indian children. The Lady Missionaries of St. Mary's with the aid of the pupils and a faithful workman are doing all the work connected with the Mission, except the financing of same. The Lady Missionaries are six in number, one of them being rather sick at the present writing.

I wonder if you could consider helping us out in our need. We need at least two accredited teachers and more other sisters. I have confidence that you will make a success of the work and make it prosper.

At present, under patronage of St. Joseph, we have all we need, except sisters, neither debts nor obligations of any kind.

St. Mary's Mission is a little over one hundred and fifty miles from your present home.

Kindly consider the matter in your prayers and try and give me a cheering answer.

(Father   Caldi   to   Rev.   Mother   Mary
Bonaventura, O.P., September 19, 1934)

No answer to this letter of Father Caldi by Mother
Bonaventura can be found. These might have been some of her
thoughts, however: How could she take over a new institution
knowing all that was expected of her sisters? Could she afford,
when she was deeply in debt with her hospitals and with the
Provincial House, to pay the high cost of room and board and of
education for her sisters, and then send them to a mission that
had not one cent left for them – she, who had not the money for a
stamp when her sisters wanted to write home?

It should be explained at this point that Mother Katherine
Drexel from the prominent and wealthy Drexel family of
Philadelphia, foundress of her own congregation of the *Sisters of
the Blessed Sacrament for Indians and Colored People*, had been
a benevolent donor to the Mission from 1905 on. In total,
Mother Katherine had spent on St. Mary's Mission for the
Colville Confederated Tribes a total of $137,631 (Records of St.
Elizabeth's Convent, Cornwell Heights, MA), more than one and
a half million dollars in today's money value.

But in 1936, Mother Katherine was 77 years of age and
stopped her contributions at the end of that same school year, in
order to provide first and foremost for all the missions she herself
had founded. Mother Katherine Drexel was canonized by Pope
John Paul II on October 1ˢᵗ, 2000.

It can be assumed that Mother Bonaventura did not know
about any arrangement whatsoever concerning Mother
Katherine's contributions. But she was very much concerned that
the first purpose of the Institute of the Poor School Sisters, to
teach the girls, be realized as soon as possible, and the good-
hearted Mother Bonaventura promised to do what she could to
help the Mission out of trouble. Permission from the
Motherhouse in Speyer was later granted, but the Dominican

congregation never obliged itself formally to have its sisters always
there.   No legal obligation with the Jesuit fathers or with the
Bishop of Spokane was ever signed.

Father Caldi, under the date of August 7, 1935, told Bishop
White, "We shall be pleased to welcome Rev. Mother M.
Bonaventura, O.P., and trust that everything here will meet her
kind approval and interest."

It was July 1, 1936 when the first Poor School Sisters moved
to St. Mary's Mission.

First, a cleaning crew went up: Sisters Eugenia, Donatilla,
Richildis, Nicasia and Metra were chosen for that task.   The
buildings at the Mission were in a state of terrible neglect.   In
1936, the following buildings were in existence: two dormitories,
one for boys and one for girls, a church, a gymnasium, the
superior's office, a school house, an old frame structure, called
"the hospital", and the main building.   The latter contained on the
first floor a chapel, sleeping quarters for some of the sisters, four
dining rooms, the kitchen and a laundry room.   Upstairs were the
sewing room, two more bedrooms, the boys' play room, the girls'
store room for their clothes and other items, and one large
storage space, containing sundry items, hardware and articles
donated by benefactors.   The sisters lived and worked in this very
old frame building from 1936-1938.

Everything they found in the old convent was in a most
primitive condition.   First, the sisters had to buy dishes; otherwise
they would have lost their appetite with what they found.   Also,
there was no place to hang clothes, and the sisters had to pound
nails into the walls of the old rooms.   They scrubbed and cleaned
for months to remove the dirt that had accumulated over the
years.   In their first missionary enthusiasm, they rose at three
o'clock in the morning to work in the fields until Father laughed
at them.

The second set of sisters to arrive at St. Mary's included Sisters Seraphica, Marina, Francis de Sales, Donatilla, Richildis, Reginalda and Aristella.

The Almighty God blessed the sisters' work in a manner visible to all. The average number of girls received during that year was sixty – a much larger number than in previous years. They were carefully trained in the regular high school subjects and also in all things that relate to domestic science, and they were given an education, which would in time form them into good Christian women.

The number of little boys received during that year and under the care of the sisters was about twenty-five. The patients received at the hospital would average about one hundred annually and they were under the constant care of the sisters.

In addition to the foregoing duties, which they had gladly assumed, the sisters took entire care of the Church: washing and keeping in perfect order the altar linens and vestments. They made all the altar bread. On occasions of great festivals, no pains were spared to make the Church most beautiful and attractive, as the Indians and many others on those occasions came to the Mission from distances of many miles. They were always pleased with the display of candles and flowers that would adorn the altar.

The sisters' labors were still not ended. They did the washing for the entire place. They did all the laundry work for the Father and the large and small boys at the Mission. They did all the washing for the hospital and, with the exception of the clothes for the girls, which they themselves would wash, all the washing for the convent. When the washing and ironing were completed, the clothes, before being returned to their respective places, were mended and put in order.

Had it not been for the sisters, the Mission would have been forced to close long before it actually did. It would not have been possible anywhere in this territory to secure the help of such services, as were rendered by the sisters, for the payment of money. The sisters came to St. Mary's Mission, knowing that they were sacrificing their lives and their health, receiving in return not a munificent salary but simply their clothing and food, some of them even buying their own clothing in order that they may not be a burden upon the Mission.

Additionally, the education of the sisters teaching at St. Mary's represented a financial burden on the Dominican community. The cost of a teacher's education and of living during the five years of study amounted from $10,000 to $12,000 for each sister. Nobody ever offered a scholarship or a reduction in education costs to the sisters working at the Mission to enable them to continue their heroic work. Only Father Balfe, Father Caldi's successor, showed himself generous in providing a small monthly allowance to the sisters.

Another great strain was lifted from the sisters when Sister Consuelo complained to Father that the sisters had absolutely no community life. Then, it was decided that the Fathers should supervise newly scheduled evening study halls.

Father Caldi expected the sisters to take care of the boys, as the Lady Missionaries had done. However, it proved to be a sheer impossibility for the sisters to teach in the classroom and, in addition, supervise the boys all day long outside of class hours and even during the nights in the dormitory. Some of the Indian boys were advanced in years and could not be properly called grade-school boys. In later years, Mother Arsinia finally had this arrangement changed as the following letter shows:

> For eleven years, our dear sisters have devoted all their energy to the worthy cause of the education and salvation of the Indian children. Most of our sisters who entered so enthusiastically upon their mission are still at St. Mary's. Very few changes have been made. The sisters are getting older and their strength is decreasing. It is especially difficult for the sisters in charge of the boys, to do justice to their religious

duties, and to enrich their teaching with the necessary preparation because the adequate supervision of the boys outside of school hours as well as in the dormitory demands every moment of their time.

It was for thirty-one years – 1936 to 1967 – that the Poor School Sisters kept on struggling courageously, under the most trying of circumstances to give to the children, and especially those poorest of God's children, the ones from broken homes, a good Christian education and a sense of security and of being wanted.

St. Mary's Mission, Omak

Mission School Band

They live in tents.

St. Mary's Fire, 1938

St. Mary's Mission and the Animal World –
by Sister Birgitta Matt, O.P., Community Archivist

Another account of life at St. Mary's Mission was written by Sister Birgitta.

Various animals are associated with the 31 years our Dominican sisters worked at St. Mary's in Omak from 1936-1967.

Sister Virginia had adopted a pet calf, which she named Boo Boo. Whenever Sister stood by the open kitchen door and called, "Boo Boo", the calf raced down the hills towards the kitchen, tail high in the air, and arrived happily at Sister Virginia's side to be treated with affection and with some goodies for his stomach.

During the 1930s, a small flock of sheep lived on the Mission grounds. Once, a ewe gave birth to two lambs. The mother ewe took care of one and rejected the second one. Sister Reginalda took the poor abandoned creature, placed him in a box near the kitchen stove, and named him Napoleon. The lamb was fed with a bottle, and it was easy to find volunteers among the children who loved to take turns in feeding little Napoleon. When the lamb was strong enough, he joined the flock of sheep on the pasture.

Then, there was the annual cattle branding. The Mission brand was a circle with a cross in the center. The calves cried when the hot iron was applied to their hides. The mama cows bellowed in pity and anger near the barnyard and almost jumped over the fence. It was difficult to keep the youngsters in their classroom seats on branding days. They wanted to be where the action was.

Snakes abounded in the nearby hills: rattlers, bull snakes and blue racers. Despite the number of these reptiles, no one ever suffered a snakebite. The Indians knew how to handle snakes and killed the poisonous ones. The designs on snake skins were attractive and the boys enjoyed draping snakeskins over their belts. The skins dried in a day or two and fell off. But there were more snakes to be caught in the hills.

The Poor School Sisters' Voices

In their stories, the sisters share their memories of those years.

Sister Fidelis, 1937: When we came to the mission, it was still an untamed country in 1937, and the community was very, very poor, in fact, as Father Benning would say, "We are roughing it." And I remember when we first came, we were cultivating the land and planting young fruit trees. One of us broke a hoe and Mother said, we just can't get another one, so we thought we couldn't buy these things over here because we never saw a store. We never went anyplace. We didn't know that it was because she didn't have any money, because she couldn't pay for it. So we wrote home that they should send hoes and hoses, things like that, because we thought we just couldn't buy that here.

And oh, just caring for all those children! They came so poor, and I had to take care of their clothes, mending their clothes, teaching them all day. After school you had them in the playroom and then, at night, we saw that they prayed. They were examined by a doctor and a nurse and everything else. It was really cute: they'd sit in a great big chair and the doctor would examine them and say, "Sister, she's got a sore ear; use olive oil" or "She has a toothache."

There were all kinds of illnesses, especially the first years, because the food was so poor and unbalanced. We were really poor and they had so many sores. Later on, Sister used hot water for their health, and that cut down on the diseases. We really saw what good food, a balanced diet and cleanliness can do for people. And after I put them to bed, I always told them a story and they always loved to hear about the Saints, and I still remember, after about two weeks, one after another of those little kids would say, "Sister, we're in a holy place." They were so overcome; it was so different from home.

I had usually about 65 children at the dorm. In the classroom we had three grades, and usually from between 40 to 65 children. I taught until 11:30 a.m., and at noon I ran down to the dining room and had to serve food for 120 children. And I remember, I had one assistant, and he helped me pour out the milk.

Sister Frances de Sales, 1933: We started school. Within 2-3 days, the children arrived. I was with the boys and taught 6th, 7th, and 8th grade. I stayed at the Mission for 12-1/2 years, usually teaching. It was very, very hard. When I came there, there was nothing, not even a shelf for the boys on which to put their suitcases. First I made shelves with old wood from barns taken down. I took a hammer and saw and cut them the right size and made shelves. Also, I made shelves in the class for the books and repaired the beds in the dormitories. The mattresses were bad, so we got old mattresses from the hospital, our own hospital. All the beds were repaired. The children had no sheets or pillowcases.

Sister Consuelo, 1933: I went to St. Mary's Mission for one year to help out, and the one year became twelve years, which were the best years of my life, the most creative. The children and I did many, many creative and beautiful things. We put on plays, which went to Spokane and won medals. They put on a little paper. We sang on the radio with the Indian children.

One day, I was in the dorm. There was a knock at the door, and in those days one never appeared in improper attire when one met a child in the middle of the night. So I dressed and the little girl at the door said, "Come, Leta has an earache" and I said, "Just a moment", and I gave her an aspirin and went back to bed. After a few moments, another knock. I dressed again and went to the door. "Sister, should I put it on her ear?" (laugh)

And one day, when I was walking from one building to the other, I was very discouraged because sometimes you saw drunken Indians. Sometimes you saw the former students come back. They had not been successful. They had not found a place in life. They had not used what we taught them. So this day, I was very, very discouraged and, walking from one building to another, a little girl put her hand in mine and said... her name was Patsy Marcela. She put her hand in mine and she said," Sister, do you like it here?" And I said, "Of course I like it here, yes, I really like it here." She said, "I do, too. It's a holy place, ain't it?" Out of the mouth of babes.

So I spent 12 years with those beautiful, simple, sensitive children who had such an enormous sense of nature and the sacred. One little girl came to me at Christmas and said, "Sister, come quick! God has a new suit on." Sister Cornelia had just put a new cloth on the altar. And the same girl said to me one day, "Sister, is today tomorrow?" We were going to go to a show in Okanogan the next day, and she couldn't wait.

One day came a truck, and on it was written PIE, for *Pacific Interurban Express* or something. It brought supplies and there was a picture of a pie on it. And one little boy said, "Sister, how come we don't get no pies? Do you guys eat all the pies?" And I thought, oh my goodness, how many children have been tortured by this idea that a pie truck comes every week and they never see any pie (laugh).

We loved to go on walks with those children. And they knew all the tracks of birds and animals. I just marveled at their knowledge of nature, their insights into the way of animals. Sometimes it could be rather vexing when you were trying seriously to teach something, and I noticed, there was restlessness in the back of the room. What's going on back there? Nothing. But there is something going on, what is going on? And you noticed there was a shirt moving violently (laugh), and in the boy's shirt or in a drawer you would open, there would be a snake, and your acceptance depended on how you reacted to that snake.

Thinking of those twelve years, the hours in the class, the hours in the dorm, the hours in the dining room, and the poverty. When I first came, there wasn't even any hot water, we had to boil the water in a cauldron in the laundry and carry it upstairs. I carried my own bath water and I carried Sister Bruenhilda's bath water. She asked me to do that for her, and it was an honor to do that for her. Then Father Balfe put hot water in, and it was a great luxury. However, his successor, Father Gleason, who eventually became Bishop Gleason, thought it was too much of a luxury. He took out the hot water. And the sicknesses we had among the children were partly due to the lack of hot water. How could we keep them clean? And Father Corkery put back the hot water, God rest his soul.

When I first came, we had 12 stoves that needed to be kept up. That meant the children, the boys, had to cut wood for our stoves and the sisters had to see to it that everyday a sufficient amount of wood would be taken to the 12 different stoves. I also remember ironing with the girls, those old fashioned irons that had to be heated on the stove, and I read them stories while they ironed. I remember reading: *The good, bad boy.* Those were good days and we really worked hard.

We did many things for each other. We served each other and loved each other. We loved the children, although we probably made many mistakes. In dealing with the Indians, we tried to teach them our sense of time, teach them our values. I know now: we did not respect the genius of their People enough. But it should be clear to all of them that went through the Mission that we really loved them.

Unidentified voices: I taught in St. Mary's Mission from 1937 to 1940. By the time I got there, our community was one year old, and the school was very primitive. The first grade children were 8, 9, 10 years old, and the upper grade children were sometimes 17, 18. I was 23, so some of them were close to my age. I had an indoor job: to make sure everyone was clean, washed at night, that they put pajamas on and slept between two sheets, not on top or below two sheets, that they got their overalls and their shoes on. We had to teach them all the primitive hygiene.

I taught the upper grades. The Indian children – the hardest subjects to teach them are geography and history. They are very good in math and grammar: they really can think. They also have a certain rhythm for dancing and singing. We put on Snow White and the Seven Dwarfs as an operetta. One sister did the music part, and I did the libretto, and the children were really talented. At that time they were not spoiled. There was no TV or radio around much, and they didn't have the feeling they had to run home all the time. And simple chores and the Mission life really appealed to them. After the war, when America became more open to many other things, the Indian children got more spoiled, too, and it got harder to deal with them at that time. During the war and before the war, it was really beautiful to teach and I really enjoyed it.

One day, Frank came howling to Sister Donatilla, with the complaint that another boy had hit him. "Where did he hit you?" Sister asked. "Between the wood shed and the kitchen."

Desautel, a town about eleven miles from St. Mary's, and East Omak were connected by a logging railroad, the tracks of which crossed part of the Mission property. Once, Sister Francis de Sales wanted to get Christmas trees and took some boys along. The boys saw the logging train coming, jumped the train, waved good-bye to the sister and disappeared. They thought it was fun, but Sister Francis de Sales didn't think it was funny at all.

Father had a hard time gathering the children back after a school break. The love of freedom in the Indian boys was strong. Also, their sense of time was different from that of a white man. Father took it in stride. "It was after two *weeks*, when you were supposed to be back – not after two moons," he would say when the delinquents finally returned.

We corrected the children with kindness and had great success. Even the adult Indians were influenced through our kind remarks. For instance, the men were induced to carry the burdens, which formerly the women had carried.

The children were always hungry. The girls would be happy if they were allowed to have their picnics with the sisters whom they all loved. Then, Mattie George would be their leader and she would always know what was good to eat. She knew where to find fresh-water clams and fish and how to roast them. The sisters always knew how to make the girls happy. Once, when the fish were roasted, Sister Rose Frances told them in broken English, "The eyes you shut and make a wish." Then, to the surprise and delight of the girls, she produced a bag of fresh baked bread from beneath her cape and proceeded to distribute large hunks of it.

What kind of food was served to the children? Meat (fish on days of abstinence), vegetable, fruit, cereal, bread, etc. Standard food, usually well prepared.

On Sundays and during holidays, the morning study hours were given to painting, drawing, penmanship and piano practice.

There was a winter that was more severe than any others. High snows came down at the end of September and stayed until May. For 6 months, all was white. Who can describe the restlessness of Indian children in a classroom if they have no place to let off steam? We had to have them either in the classrooms or in the dorms after school hours.

Days at St. Mary's Mission – Sister Consuelo Fissler, O.P.

The following are excerpts from a letter, written by Sister Consuelo Fissler, O.P., and from a report, written by Charles DePoe, Executive Secretary of the Business Council of the Colville Confederate Tribes, in 1954.

From the letter:

A thousand memories of our beloved St. Mary's Mission have been dancing through my thoughts. I thought of the twelve happy years I spent at St. Mary's (1948-1960) and the joy I had in teaching. I recalled the eagerness of the students, their clear singing voices and extraordinary gifts in artistic expression.

From the report:

On April 30, 1954, a committee from the Business Council, consisting of Nellie Rims, Louis Orr, Harry Owl, Henry Covington and Superintendent Phillips, made a special visit to St. Mary's Mission. What started out to be a routine business survey, turned out to be a delightful excursion, full of surprises and pleasantries.

After a briefing by Father Corkery, our genial host, we visited the 7th and 8th grade classroom where they were in the midst of demonstrating "how to figure interest on loans." The committee, along with the writer of this report, was completely baffled by the speed and accuracy, which the boys and girls demonstrated in working out the problems on the blackboard.

In all the other classes that we visited during the day, we received the same surprises. The courtesy and respect that the children showed to their teachers and to us was something that I thought had died some time ago. But here, at St. Mary's Mission, they are very much alive and practiced every minute of the day.

There is a spirit of willingness and helpfulness in the attitude of the students, and a desire to learn and to be a useful citizen.

It was near lunchtime when our footsteps led us toward the dining hall. Little did we know that we were in for a very delightful surprise by the home economics class. We were served a full-course banquet by Sally Swan, Agnes George and Lorraine Robinette, under the supervision of Sister Theresianna.

Our next stop was the exhibit of the sewing classes. Some of the work that seemed to be exceptionally beautiful was done by Sally Swan, Darlene Quill, Martina Pichette, and Wanda Rose Andrews. But then, all the work was very beautiful.

The Sister teachers all have Life Certificates to teach. The school is accredited and the standards are kept up to par. In talking over the tour, we were in agreement that you (the teachers and children) are all doing wonderful work and that we are for you 100 per cent.

The Children's Voices

Paschal Sherman, A.B., A.M., PhD., LL.B., M.P.L., after whom St. Mary's Mission is named today, was Father De Rougé's most scholarly student, a full-blooded Indian who later worked for the Federal Veteran Administration in Washington, D.C. His is the most distinguished voice in a questionnaire developed by Sister Ilma M. Raufer, O.P., for her 1966 publication *Black Robes and Indians on the Last Frontier*:

In my senior year, I won a Knights of Columbus graduate scholarship at Catholic University, Washington, D.C., in an international competitive examination. I could not have won except for the education obtained at the Mission, with the concomitant sharpening of my perception and wits, because the tests included Latin, French, English and ancient history, on which I obtained very little additional learning. Indeed, with no additional French courses taken at University, I passed the German and French tests for the Ph.D. degree some years later at the Catholic University.

Of course, the classes at the Mission have produced more notable representatives. William F. Hill required only about two years at St. Martin's College, Lacey, Washington to earn an A.B. degree and later he became a public figure in county and state cattle associations, as a county commissioner, as Democratic committeeman in state politics, and in civic activities.

Peter Campbell finished his architectural degree at the Catholic University.

Mission educators are also proud of the achievements of Moses George, who came to the Mission as a little boy. He became a road-building engineer with headquarters at Wenatchee, Washington. He learned the use of the transit in surveying, and the principles of road engineering virtually on his own and turned out to be a high official in this field in the state of Washington.

Sammy Smith, one of the three Smith brothers at the school, became immensely wealthy in cattle operations.

John B. Cleveland also became a public figure in state politics and in civic activities and is noted as a forceful and effective speaker.

Ross Hilleary is a successful farmer in the Coeur d'Alene region of Idaho, and the late Louie Smitkin, some years ago, was in the trucking business and a baseball great in Okanogan county.

Sister Ilma Raufer's publication also makes mention of Mr. Chris C. Smith of Bridgeport, Washington. To her question, "How, do you think, did the education the Mission offered help to raise the living standards of the different tribes involved?" he answered, "It helped to prepare the young people to find their place in the White man's society. Unscrupulous Whites, some merchants, would not let an Indian alone until they got almost all of their treaty money."

Mr. De Vos has the following to say, "While attending the 1959 Indian celebration at Nespelem, I made it my business to talk with all the Indians I could find who had attended St. Mary's. With only one exception, all, male or female, were strong in their praise of the benefits they had received. Many of this generation had found it possible to leave the reservation and integrate into better homes and living conditions. It gave me real joy."

And last but not least, an excerpt from a letter from Mrs. Ruby Babcock who attended St. Mary's as an eighth grader and pays tribute to the inner values instilled at the Mission.

Life did seem luxurious to us there. The people of the vicinity were Depression poor. None of the houses had any more than well water and felt fortunate if they had that. But we were very lonely at times. My memories are not so much of the every day living there, as of the contrast between the spiritual poverty we had been raised in and the wonderful truths that we learned at the Mission. We were among those unfortunate children who are allowed to grow up too soon. We were very wise in the ways of the world by the time we attended St. Mary's. I remember many times, as a child, wondering just what this life was all about and feeling an uneasiness and restlessness in my ignorance. We did learn that there must be discipline of the soul. I have always looked back on my year at St. Mary's as the holiest year of my life. Not that I was holy, but that for the first time I lived with people who were close to God – people who were goodness itself.

The Fires

Two big fires wreaked havoc at St. Mary's Mission: the first one in 1919, and the second in 1938. The summer climate is very hot and dry, and the danger of brush and wild fires springs up every year. Of course wooden buildings in such an area are especially in danger.

In the 1919 fire, the old boys' school was the only building on the grounds of the Mission to go up in flames. The fire was so controlled that it did not spread to other buildings, due to Father de Rougé's wisdom to greatly insolate the various buildings on campus. However, the loss of his famous school was total, not many items were saved. Gone was the famous museum, the library with over 2000 books, which constituted in those pioneer days a great treasure, and all the school equipment. Destroyed also was another historical treasure: the correspondence Father de Rougé had received.

When the second fire broke out, the Poor School Sisters were running the Mission school. On Sunday, the Feast of St. Ignatius of Loyola, the 31ˢᵗ of July, 1938, they had just put the last jars of canned apricots in the cellars and felt a certain relief after weeks of hard work. Fresh cinnamon rolls and bread were baking. The heat was intense in the old kitchen and the stovepipe was red-hot from working overtime. The heat from the canning together with the heat of the season must have been too much, and a fire sparked in the old chimney, which had known more than one blaze.

In a few minutes, the two-story building stood in raging flames. People working in nearby fields came and picked up three heavy statues from the chapel and threw them in the water of the swimming pool, in order to douse water on the flames. Sister Donatilla hurled two bales of veil and habit material from the sewing room windows to the outside. They landed near the

Statue of St. Michael, a few feet from the inferno. Everything else in the building was doomed.

The fire fighters from Omak and Desautel came too late. But they soaked the walls and the roof of the girls' dormitory, which was near the chapel, in order to save it. Their attempts were successful. Sister Donatilla and Virginia sat on the two bales, saved from the sewing room, and the latter said, "I hope the wind drives the flames towards the cemetery and not the chicken house. Everyone at the cemetery is dead anyway, but we need the chickens and the eggs." Actually, this is what happened.

Once the building had collapsed in the fire, the flames, stirred by the wind, moved towards the cemetery and burned themselves out in the dry weeds.

Father Joseph Balfe was on his way to Omak when he heard the sirens scream and was told that his Mission was on fire. This is how Father Joseph Balfe would tell the story:

About half past nine, Saturday morning, we saw dense smoke pouring out through the roof of the kitchen. As fast as we could, we got a ladder, a hoe and an axe, and the hired man climbed to the roof. He could do very little because by that time the flames had broken through the shingles in two or three places, and it was far too hot to get close enough to cut through so that we might douse water into the space between the roof and the ceiling. The water pressure was low, very low (it had been an unusual year, no rain since April) so there was not much help from there.

The kitchen was located near the center of the service building which includes, besides the kitchen, all the dining rooms, the sisters' quarters, laundry, cellar, two classrooms and the chapel. The wind was not very strong, but in spite of that, the fire rapidly spread both north and south along the line of the building and, within thirty minutes, the entire service building was either ablaze or melting down in a terrific heat. In fact, within an hour's time the building had taken the outline of a ruin, and that is what it is today.

The fire department from Omak, seven miles away, had sent up a truck and some men and, later on, a truckload of C.C.C. boys came. With this help we did something to prevent the fire spreading to nearby outhouses. Twice, the little shed, which houses our light plant, caught fire from the intense heat and the showers of sparks and flying embers, but we fought the blaze down, so the plant is safe and is working all right. A long line of woodsheds with a good deal of wood burnt up, as did some farm machinery, which we parked in a shed not far from the laundry.

The chapel was the last building to go on the south end of the doomed line. We saved the vestments, except our Benediction cope, the organ (two old Indians climbed to the choir loft for that), a few other things and, of course, the Blessed Sacrament, but aside from those articles, the chapel sank into ashes.

Here is what caused comment from people who later viewed the ruins. The girls' dormitory was built jam up against the chapel - that is, about five feet of one sidewall of the dormitory touched the chapel. Blazing brands and embers fell constantly on the tin roof and stuccoed sides of the dormitory, but in spite of the fact that we had to watch a somewhat dangerous porch at the rear of the dormitory, that building never caught fire, and it is there today, sound and cool and unmarked, practically as if there had been no fire. So we have that building, thank the Lord, and also the administration building, where my office is located, another fireproof building nearby, which houses two classrooms, the boys' dormitory, and the gymnasium.

The loss is considerable, especially the loss of the contents of the burnt building. All kitchen equipment was destroyed, as was that of the laundry, dining rooms, sisters' quarters, (the sisters saved only what they wore), the girls' classroom equipment, and what was in the chapel, excepting what I have mentioned as salvaged. The sisters had canned a good deal of apricots from our own orchards, but the fruit and jars melted down.

Today the water reservoir is still burning. Fire got into the sawdust insulation between the tank and the outer protecting wall, and the smoldering heat burst the bricks out in so many places that the whole thing will have to be rebuilt.

The sisters are getting reorganized down in the gymnasium, as well as they can, and although we cannot be sure just what is best to do yet, most likely, if quarters are re-established for them, it will be there in the gymnasium.

The War Years

While the sisters took care of the Indian Mission in Omak and, also, spread from there to take on other hospitals and schools and build new ones, there was a war raging in Europe. Letters were found from Germany, describing the terrors that were endured at the motherhouse in Speyer and by the sisters' individual families.

-- From the Dominican Publication *A Measure of Leaven.*

The Second World War added sharply to the separation our sisters felt, far from home and family. From Hitler's attack on Poland on September 1, 1939, until Pearl Harbor, December 7, 1941, all mail to and from Germany was censored. From 1941, until the war ended, messages to Germany, sent via the International Red Cross, could only be 25 words long. "We agonized", recalled Sister Birgitta, "over how to say the most with such few words."

And they worried about their families' welfare. "They had nothing," Sister Birgitta said.

The war caused hardships for the Poor School Sisters here in the United States, as well. Recent arrivals and others without American citizenship were declared enemy aliens. They had to report monthly to the authorities and carry alien identification.

Rationing of meat, butter, sugar, oil, coffee, canned food, shoes and gasoline made running the convent, the school and the hospitals difficult. It was impossible to construct so much as a shed. If a washer, heater, stove, or clock broke, there were no replacements.

Sister Consuelo, 1933: One of the most poignant aspects of the second WW was that it came so suddenly, so soon after our arrival. We were not at home, and we had no friends in this country. We had not even begun to become part of this new world. We were really foreigners. And one thing, which stands out in my mind, is that we were fingerprinted like criminals, although in retrospect I think we were treated much more gently than the Japanese. We were not put into camps. We were not told to go back to Germany. We were allowed to stay here, but we were fingerprinted.

So we were in this new land, homeless as far as the country was concerned. This country was at war with our own homeland, where our relatives lived and were dying and were refugees. Our mothers died during these years when we had no communication. It was great suffering, which we bore and, I believe, it was only in retrospect that it was really unfathomable. It was unimaginable. If today a war broke out between Germany and the United States, I could bear it because I am at home here. And as long as there was a just cause I would be wholeheartedly on the side of the Americans. But in those days, although I realized Hitler should not win nor could have won, it was still my country and those were still my brothers and sisters, and when I saw the newsreels I closed my eyes. You know in those days they were always played before movies. I could not bear to look at them.

Sister Marina: When the WWII started, we were cut off; we couldn't even write a letter home, only through the Red Cross, a few lines. We didn't even know if our relatives were still living.

Meanwhile in Germany, Hitler's agents were carefully guarding the German borders, lest any money would be smuggled across to Holland, Switzerland or any other neighboring country. The motherhouse in Speyer owned a house near Geneva, Switzerland, which, because of poor income, had to be supported from the German motherhouse. Sister Alexandra, in her capacity as the bursar of the St. Ingbert mission, sent money at regular intervals to Switzerland. She continued to do so after the Nazi government had passed the new *Devisengesetze* – currency laws – not knowing of the serious consequences involved.

When Sister Alexandra realized she had by ignoring the laws put the Gestapo on her heels, she fled to Switzerland and from there embarked the liner *Conte di Savoia*, which brought her via Geneva-New York to the safety of the United States in October, 1936. The poor refugee never quite recovered from the terrible experiences she had been through. She spent six years in the quiet solitude of Our Lady of the Valley where she subsequently died on September 2, 1942. She was the first of the sisters to be buried at the newly laid out cemetery of Our Lady of the Valley.

Several of the sisters' American houses received telephone calls from unidentified persons, asking whether there was a Sister Alexandra in residence.

The presence of the refugee made it impossible for Mother Bonaventura to travel to Germany for the General Chapter in Speyer, in 1937. On January 30, 1937, Mother Bonaventura wrote a letter to Charles D. White, Bishop of Spokane:

> Our General Chapter in Speyer will meet on March 7, for the election of a Mother General. I am in great doubt as to what I should do. In Germany, they are expecting me. Here in America, all of our sisters are opposed to my going to Germany in these troubled times. They fear I would be kept as a

hostage for Sister Alexandra, our refugee from
Germany. The sisters suspect that the German
government has been informed through its expansive
spy system that Sister Alexandra is with us.

The Bishop answered on February 3, 1937:

> Taking into consideration all that you have written
> me about the hazards of your attending that meeting,
> I advise you not to go.
>
> Owing to the present persecution of the Church
> in Germany, the attendant government censorship of
> mail, and the efficient spy system, you have no means
> of discussing with Mother General the reasons for
> your not attending. I feel sure that if Mother General
> knew your reasons, she would not want you to attend
> the Chapter.

Letters written in German from the Motherhouse in Speyer
talk about war terrors in Germany. In translation they read as
follows:

Speyer, Feast of Mary's Devotement, 1944

> My dear Sisters, when this letter reaches you
> many of you will already have heard of the horrible
> tragedy that our nursing home in Münchweiler had to
> endure. On Thursday afternoon, Nov. 15, the sisters'
> house fell victim to an enemy attack. Two bombs hit
> the house. All of the occupants were buried alive
> under the rubble with the exception of Sister Franka
> who was praying in the chapel. Thanks to God's love
> and care and the immediate help of the Münchweiler

people, Sister Floriana, Sister Hildis, Sister
Sepulchra, Sister Lusina, Sister Gratia und one of the
two sisters of the nursing home were saved before late
evening. Sister Liebgid and the other nursing home
sister were not found. The eleven older individuals
that had made a home at the Münchweiler house,
and also a six months old infant, fell prey to the
attack.

As soon as the access problems were half way
resolved, Mother Prioress Helmtrudis and I drove
with His Excellency, the Reverend Bishop, to the site
of the disaster. There was only a pile of rubble left.
Fortunately, the sisters that were saved are out of
danger. Sister Gratia and Sister Ilidis are in the
hospital at Rodalben. Sister Gratia with broken arms
and legs, also many head injuries, Ilidis with countless
bruises and burn injuries on her face.

The greatest sorrow is the death of our dear Sister
Liebgid. On Saturday morning, the brave rescue
efforts of the men only recovered her dead body.
How often had she said during those last days, "You'll
see, I will die under the rubble", and it literally
became her destiny. All of us, who were there when
her body was recovered, won't forget the sight. She
was not mutilated, only showed the signs of being
buried. But what moved us to our deepest souls was
her posture in death: her head inclined to the right,
the fingers of her right hand seemingly making the
sign of a vow. Involuntarily, I had to think of the
statue of the Holy Cecilia of Maderna that shows the
corpse of the Holy Martyr in that same position and
it, also had been found that way in the catacombs.

Sister Liebgid died under the rubble. Her only wish that she mentioned again and again to her fellow sisters during the last days before her death was, "If I could only renew Profession, then I would die happily." It was not granted to her to kneel before the altar on December 8th. The Lord took home his bride beforehand. But surely He heard her plea for the grace of Profession even in death. The debris of the house was the altar of Profession, on which she laid her hand in vow, dying. Her devotion was sealed with her blood.

Speyer, March 25th, 1946

Dear Mother Arsenia!

I'm sure you would like to know how we're doing here. We are in great destitution because of the lack of food. During the winter, we only received two tons of pressed coal dust for heating, so it was impossible to keep the house warm. Only a few furnaces in some of the rooms that were heated with wood could keep the sisters at least a little warm. We used the Kindergarten facilities as a warm-up room for all. Sister Rosamunde often said, "Maybe one of these days a plane will drop a package in our garden, from our dear sisters in America."

You cannot even begin to imagine the hardships and misery in our destroyed Fatherland. The way the cities look: Ludwigshafen, Kaiserslautern, Pirmasens, Homburg and Zweibrücken! Many smaller towns have also been afflicted, especially along the French border. Many hardships, much distress, great famine and abundance of illnesses are haunting our German people. But our faith in God's help is steadfast. He, who has rescued us so wonderfully during the hardships of war, will surely help us along now. We are bravely awaiting the future!

With my most affectionate wishes and blessings for you, dear Mother Arsenia, and all our dear Sisters I remain faithfully Yours,

M. Edeltaud Weimar

After the war ended in 1945, packages of food and clothing up to 22 pounds were allowed for relief of the starving Europeans. Despite their meager resources and the responsibility of their missions, the sisters responded with great fervor to the needs of their German sisters and relatives.

In two years, they sent 1,411 parcels to the motherhouse in Speyer, along with bales of habit and veil fabric. In addition, they sent packages to more than 100 missions, and each sister sent a monthly parcel to members of her own family.

Sister Birgitta, 1928: Many of us did not eat candy or cookies in those years. We saved all sweets to add them to our parcels of love.

Unidentified Voices: After the war was over, we received word from Germany. During those years there was no communication with Germany. We didn't know if our people were still alive or not. Finally, the first letters came in, and they told us who had died and who was still alive. And then, naturally, we got some news from over there, and every letter told us the same misery and poverty and the real starvation that the sisters went through. And many of our sisters were ill. They were very anemic due to undernourishment and not having the proper food for so many years.

As soon as we heard of the possibility of sending them packages, we all decided, we will all do with very little for ourselves. We will be satisfied with anything we have, so we could save some money and send things to them. Sister Laritana was appointed to make packages for Speyer and the sisters over there, and we decided to have applesauce every morning for our food, for breakfast, instead of having one or two changes during the week as we used to for a while. And Sister Laritana was busy for weeks and weeks, day and night, making packages. She made them by the dozen. Every week, one or two truck loads would be delivered to Kettle Falls to be shipped over, and in the hospitals in Chewelah and Tonasket, they also decided not to build or expand the place or make any expensive repairs until this urgent need in Germany was over. So this money was saved to be used as postage and transportation for our packages. And when we learned from Germany: it was really touching when the first letters came in, telling us, "You have saved our lives." Sister Rosamunda said she had just dreamed the night before an airplane was coming into the garden and had landed there and had popped out packages, and the very next day packages were delivered by mail. We had shipped some vitamins and some canned meat, some of the necessities. Sister Petronlia was so anemic that the doctors said this saved her life.

Privately, you could send a small package, about 5-8 pounds. I sent a little package with soap. It was the hospital soap, the small bars, and I sent them over to a convent of 60 sisters. It arrived there on the 2nd of February, and they wrote back to me, "You should have heard the hallowing in this room today. It was purification day. We had not seen soap for so many years and today each one found a bar of soap at their place. You cannot imagine what it meant to us."

Mother Bonaventura Groh, R.I.P.

The sisters in the Pacific Northwest faced their greatest sorrow in 1942. On September 23, after a short illness, Mother Bonaventura died, just short of her 65th birthday. Everybody thought, losing her, who was the Mother of all, irrevocably broke the heart of the American province. It was Mother Bonaventura who founded the American Mission by virtue of her intellectual prowess, the strength of her faith and her steadfastness. She was also the one who led the Poor School Sisters to their important role and their standing in the Pacific Northwest. Her memory lives on in her old and her new Fatherland. Her grave under the big Cross in Kettle Falls became the Sisters' most favorite place to pray.

In her Community History, Sister Birgitta included the following obituary:

Mother M. Bonaventura Groh, O.P.   R.I.P.
(1877-1942)

For there abide faith, hope and charity,
but the greatest of them is CHARITY.
1.Cor. 13, 13.

Ave Maria!

Dear Sisters,

A door has opened. Our dear Mother's soul passed through it. The door was closed again. We would have liked to follow her beyond the sacred threshold. But the entrance is barred to us.

We are plunged in deepest grief. Yet, we will not grieve as those who have no hope. Mother went to her eternal reward. In the home, where we all expect to go, she is praying for us and waiting to meet us again.

Our dear Mother has left behind no written testament. Her example and her words furnish one that is deeply engraved in our hearts. Each of us has individual memories of our beloved Mother. Let us cherish them, and ponder over them.

Utter sacrifice of self and charity were her most outstanding virtues. No matter how exhausted she often was, she still found time to pay attention to the various needs and diverse wants of her sisters.

Our small community has had a great Foundress. Her body was given back to the earth from whence it came. Her soul, united with God, keeps watch over us, so that her work may go on. May she delight to see us faithful bearers of the torch she handed to us: the torch of love of God and fellow men.

Ex umbris et imaginibus in veritatem - From shadows and imaginations into reality. His Excellency, The Most Reverend Charles D. White, our Bishop of Spokane, quoted these words from Cardinal J.H. Newman's tombstone in his eulogy at the last rites for our dear Mother. The words we are using in her praise are also shadows and mere images of her life's work.

Yes, a door has opened. We realized the truth of death and eternity, while the door stood ajar. We will walk as worthy children of so great a Mother in this land of shadows. Then God's reality shall be ours.

Mother Bonaventura was born on September 29, 1877 in Rodalben, in the German Palatinate. She was 13 years old, when she entered the Dominican Order as a postulant and student of the convent high school and later the normal school. After finishing her scientific and monastical education, she worked as an assistant nurse in St. Ingbert, Eppenbrunn, Lautzkirchen and Landstuhl. After leaving for the New World as the Reverend Mother of the Poor School Sisters, she adapted quickly to the foreign culture and customs and established the American Missions with a sure hand. Her clarity of mind and her willpower were paired with a heroic capability for suffering and inexhaustible kindheartedness. Her work continues to live and to prosper.

In her name, may we consider ourselves as the children of one world that embraces all people and all races in the love of Jesus Christ. Amen.

Mother Bonaventura's grave can still be found at the Our Lady of the Valley cemetery. However, the property is a private residence today.

Epilogue

The Poor School Sisters in Spokane, Washington – History Concluded

The history of the Dominican Sisters didn't end here. As a matter of fact – as one can see from the attached American history of the order – a lot of their school and hospital work has not been mentioned here or had not yet begun. And the Sisters might feel that their greatest undertaking and achievement in the Pacific Northwest is missing from this account altogether: the foundation and building of *Holy Family Hospital* in Spokane, Washington.

On August 31,1944, Mother Arsenia Stalter purchased a 16-block parcel on Spokane's north side for $13,500, but it was not for 16 years that the hospital was built. The first step was *Holy Family Home*, an 80-bed convalescent home, costing $1,144,898, completed on May 31, 1960. But the north side community still wanted a hospital. The goal was large: $3,600,000. Every penny was saved and put aside for *Holy Family Hospital*. But a loan was necessary and, on August 29, 1964, a 138-bed facility – built on time and under budget – came to dedication. A four-day open house the following weekend attracted 30,000 visitors and caused a huge traffic jam. In 1989, at the time of its 25-year anniversary, the hospital had been expanded four times.

Yet, new horizons still lay ahead. The sisters' two ministries, health care and education, were in the midst of a revolution. The sisters' response to their declining numbers was to extend their services.

Myriam's House began in 1986 to provide a supportive residence for women recovering from abuse, addiction, divorce, or any life crisis.

In 1990, the Dominican Outreach board's response to homeless single women and their children was the foundation of the *Transitional Living Center* (TLC) with 15 apartments, a sense of community, comprehensive support services and specialized child care.

The *Women's Drop-In Center* opened its doors in 1991, providing downtown outreach, support groups and life skills classes, free for all women attending.

In February of 1995, after 70 years of independence, the Poor School Sisters of St. Dominic closed their community in the Pacific Northwest and joined the Sinsinawa Dominicans, based in Wisconsin. At that time, in 1995, of the 36 remaining Poor School Sisters, 20 were from Germany. Most are retired and are allowed to live out their retirement, as long as they wish, at the Dominican Center of Spokane.

Myriam's House mission statement spells out some of the priorities of the Poor School Sisters' work:

Humbly aware that a merciful God has given to us in abundance, and compelled by the Gospel call to justice, we, women religious of Spokane, commit ourselves to share the resources held among us to assist women in their struggle toward wholeness. We dedicate ourselves to create, and continuously recreate a home environment that will nourish body / heart / spirit of those who journey with us. We will, with God's help, empower women in transition to move steadfastly and gracefully through times of crises to new life.

History of the Poor School Sisters of St. Dominic: Overview of the American Foundation

1925 10 sisters & 1 postulant (fledgling nun) leave from Speyer, Germany to Helena, Montana. Served for 36 years.

Superior and Foundress Sister Bonaventura Groh,
Arsenia Stalter,
Walburgis Mayers,
Virginia Mathieu,
Jucunda Eichenlaub,
Clodia Joerg,
Eugenia Schneider,
Mitis Weissenmayer,
Gallena Klomann,
Gisela Germann and
Postulant Hedwig Friebe (returned in 1927)

1928	9 new sisters from Germany
1929	Took over *St. Mary's Hospital*, Conrad, Montana
1930	Opened *St. Joseph's Hospital*, Chewelah, Washington
1930-34	12 new sisters from Germany
1931	Settled at *Our Lady of the Pines*, a farm in Chewelah
1934	Moved to abandoned Mission in Ward, Washington, near Kettle Falls, *Our Lady of the Valley Convent*. 32 sisters by now.

1936-37	22 new sisters from Germany, Ages 16 – 20, totaling 54
1936	Took over *St. Mary's Indian Mission.*, Omak, Washington
1937	Built new *St. Mary's Hospital*, Conrad, Montana
1937	Opened *Siena Club*, residence for single women, Helena, Montana
1938	9 new sisters from Germany
1938	Opened *St. Martin's Hospital* in Tonasket, Washington. 76 sisters by now.
1939	Purchased *Mount Carmel Hospital* in Colville, Washington
1942	On September 23, Mother Bonaventura died
1943	Purchased *Mount Carmel* Annex
1943	Added new wing to *St. Joseph's Hospital*, Chewelah
1944	Purchased 40 acres in Spokane, Washington
1945	Opened *St. Dominic's Convent*, a house of studies, in Spokane, Washington
1947	Opened *St. William's School* in Shelby, Montana
1948	Opened new school in Cutbank, Montana
1954	Moved *St. William's School* to new building. Former school became new convent.
1955	Built new convent in Shelby
1956/57	Built *Thomas Hall* with print shop, gymnasium & classrooms at *Our Lady of the Valley Convent*
1958	Opened *Assumption School*, a new parish in Spokane
1960	Built *Holy Family Nursing Home* in Spokane
1962	Opened *St. Thomas More School*, a new parish in Spokane.
1931-63	69 American women entered the Community
1964	Built *Holy Family Hospital* adjacent to Holy Family Nursing Home, Spokane

1969   Built new Provincial House in Spokane. *Our Lady of the Valley* was sold.

1970   Managed new *Pondera County Hospital* in Conrad, Montana, to replace the old St. Mary's Hospital.

1970   Added two more floors to *Holy Family Hospital* in Spokane

1979   Created *Dominican Health Services*, hospital corporation

1983   Built new *St. Joseph's Hospital* in Chewelah

1985   Started *DominiCare* in Steven's County

1986   Sponsored *Miryam's House*, the first women's shelter, in Spokane

1986   Sponsored *Holy Family Adult Day Health Program*

1986   Separated from Speyer Congregation, Germany

1988   Formed *Dominican Network* for the three hospitals

1988   Formed *Dominican Outreach Foundation*

1989   Built *St. Joseph's Long Term Care* adjacent to the hospital in Chewelah

1990   Added new wing to *Mt. Carmel Hospital* in Colville

1993   Opened *Transitional Living Center, TLC*, another women's shelter, in Spokane

1994   Formed new corporation for TLC, Miryam's House and Drop-in-Center, the three women's shelters in Spokane, together with the Sinsinawa Dominicans, Providence Sisters, Holy Names Sisters and the Franciscan Sisters

1995   Dominican Sisters of Spokane merge with the Sinsinawa Sisters from Wisconsin

Short Overview of the History of the Institute of the Poor School Sisters, Sisters of the Third Order of Penance of St. Dominic, in Speyer, Germany

Mother Bonaventura's Diary, 1925

1. Speyer, on the Rhine River

On the middle reaches of the legendary, hotly contended, glorious Rhine River, on the left banks, lays the old imperial city of Speyer. Speyer has a history unlike any other German city. Many times, the history of the people, as well as the history of the Church, played out within her walls.

Speyer was built by the Romans long Before Christ. Remains from that time are the *Altpörtel* – old gate - and the *Heidentürmchen* – little heathen tower. Already in the 4th century, Speyer was made *Bischofsstadt* – city of Bishops. Oftentimes, Speyer was the scene of bloody wars. In the Thirty-Year War, all of the Palatinate and Speyer specifically were heavily beleaguered. Afterwards, the country didn't suffer any less under Ludwig XIV from France, whose commander, Mélac, burnt Speyer down. The city also didn't escape later wars.

Even the calamitous Reformation cast her shadow on the imperial city. In 1526, and again in 1529, the German *Kaiser* – emperor - called the German Sovereigns to the *Reichstag* – parliament – to Speyer. The Lutheran sovereigns protested against this call; hence the name "Protestants". At the present time, almost half of Speyer's citizens are Protestants. They also took over some of the Catholic Churches. The *Retscher* church, which was built about 1000 B.C., represents a monumental protest of the divided.

2.   The Speyer Dome

The Speyer Dome is the oldest Church building on the Rhine River and also the largest dome in Germany. The imposing structure is a masterpiece of early Romanic architecture. The German Kaiser Konrad II himself laid the foundation in 1030. The dome was consecrated in 1060, but the building was completed only in 1135. The illustrious Cathedral was destined to become the burial place of the German Kaiser. In the crypt, eight German emperors, three empresses and one princess await their resurrection on Judgment Day. The Bishops of the diocese are also interred in the dome.

In the high dome, Saint Bernhard preached a crusade around the year 1146. Upon entering the dome, the choir sung the *Salve Regina*, when finishing, Saint Bernhard added the words, *"O clemens, o pia, o dulcis Virgo Maria!"*

During the almost nine hundred years of its existence, the dome went through changing times and fate, including lightening strikes and fire. But always the building was restored, and it was newly consecrated in 1822. King Ludwig I fitted its every wall with multicolored murals.

3.   Monasteries in the Palatinate

Just like the German people in general had a deep relationship with their monasteries, so had the Speyer diocese. In the Speyer area, there were 38 monasteries for men and 23 for women, belonging to different Orders. From these, 12 monasteries were in the old imperial city alone: 10 for men and 2 for women. The 60 Palatinate monasteries all fell prey to the swaying of time: the last 15 to the secularization conducted by the French during the 18th Century, along the left banks of the Rhine River. All monasteries ceased to exist, with the exception of St.

Magdalena in Speyer.   Even St. Magdalena was moribund in 1802, but arose to live anew and lively.

4. St. Magdalena

The most important dates of its history are the following:

Around   1228   Foundation

            1304   Conversion to the Dominican Order

            1689   Destruction of the monastery and burning of the city

Around   1700   Reconstruction

        1792-1793   Repeated escape of sisters from the French imperial Army

            1802   Abolishment of the monastery by the French.   Some of the sisters purchased the monastery buildings to live there and protect them in the hope that some day the monastery would be established again.

            1816   Foundation of an educational institute for girls

            1826   Permission by King Ludwig I to resurrect the monastery

            1828   Ceremonious grand opening of the monastery and take-over of the Catholic Speyer girls' school

            1892   Construction of the new convent.   (The writer of this entered in 1890 and has witnessed the erection of the building.)   The nuns' actions were considered very beneficially for Speyer, as well as for the whole diocese.

The Institute of the Poor School Sisters derived from the St. Magdalena monastery.

5. Institute of the Poor School Sisters

The Most Reverend Bishop of Speyer, N. Weiß, perceived the need for sisters to teach the female youth of the diocese. In 1852, the Bishop, together with the Reverend Mother Mathilde Königsberger, Prioress of the St. Magdalena monastery, founded the Institute of the Poor School Sisters of the 3rd Order [not cloistered, sic] of the Penance of St. Dominic. For the time being, the St. Magdalena monastery was supposed to be the motherhouse for those sisters. Together with the nuns at the monastery, they received training for their religious, as well as their teaching professions.

The daughter congregation prospered, specifically under the knowledgeable leadership of the merited Reverend Mother M. Bonifatia v. Besnard (1883-1907). The rapid growth of trainees at the Institute made a separation from the monastery necessary. Bishop v. Ehrler appointed the first vicar of the Poor School Sisters, Sister M. Caecilia Ehrhardt. She rendered outstanding services to the Institute.

The new Institute further flourished under the guidance of the following sisters:

1st Prioress, Mother M. Ignatia
In 1907, Sister M. Ignatia was elected first Prioress of the Institute of the Poor School Sisters. To her fell the gigantic task to:
1) build the Institute's own motherhouse,
2) obtain corporation permission and
3) attain administrative permission for a normal school.

Resolute and diplomatic at the same time, and in the face of many conflicts and difficulties, Mother Ignatia was successful in completing all three tasks.   In the best location of the city's southwest arose a magnificent building, designed by the renowned architect Perignon – our motherhouse.   Architect Perignon had visited and studied famous monasteries in Germany and France. Similar to those, he built our new motherhouse within one year. Although it looks like a medieval cloister, our motherhouse meets all the demands of our modern time.

The move from St. Magdalena to the new motherhouse was made in 1910. Holy St. Joseph became the new patron; and from then on both motherhouses were separate.

A very special commemoration be devoted to our good, self-sacrificing sisters of the first hour.   They were the venerable Sisters Dominica, Constantia, Ignatia, Felicitas, Magdalena, Laurentia, Martha, Theresia, Mechtildis, Aloysia, Clothildis, Remigia, Columba, Rosalia, Paula, Placida, Cornelia, Hildegard, Benedicta, Zitta, Lidwina, Melania, Monika [and Bonaventura, the writer of this history, sic].

We received the appropriate three-year teacher training that was required at that time and took over the diverse Catholic girl schools of the diocese where our work was blessed by the Holy God.   Poverty is our Holy virtue, and the sisters were exceedingly poor.   Their teachers' salary was minimal.   Meat dishes were a rarity.   Throughout all of their lives, on Saturdays, many of the good sisters not only abstained from meat but also from fruit, out of love to our most blessed Virgin.   Some sisters satisfied their hunger with bread crusts that had been thrown out by the children.   What a wonderful spirit of abjuration and asceticism!   It is from this profound fundament that our Institute developed; our new motherhouse is built on its secure basis.

Mother Ignatia, the first Prioress of our Institute, possessed an admirable creative power that cannot be emulated.   She died after a long, hard time in her sickbed.

Sister Constantia

Where Mother Ignatia persevered in the severe exercise of Holy Poverty, Siser Constantia persisted steadily in the spirit of prayer. Our sisters were ennobled with prayer as part of their fundamental nature. Sister Constantia, Matron of St. Ingbert for fifty years, did not miss one Holy Mass. Most often, she attended two, although Church was ten minutes away and she had difficulties walking. She filled the last years of her life exclusively with praying.

Her specific intentions within her continuous prayers were her plea for good priests and that the sisters – while doing their duties – may only think of the Glory of God and the salvation of the immortal souls. When we were allowed some better pay and our financial woes dissipated, the good Mother worried that the sisters might abandon the path of Holy Poverty and become wasteful. Henceforth, that was the particular subject of her prayers. Living wholly within the spirit of belief herself, her steady quest was to show the sisters to accept everything that happened in their daily lives with that same spirit of belief. Because of her rich life experience and her wisdom, her advice was much valued and appreciated. Such was the spirit of most of our first sisters.

Sister Placida

Sister Placida was called "the Sister after Jesus' Heart". She was the novice master of the Institute, an important task, which Sister Monica had before her.

Sister Monika

The Reverend Dominican Father, M. Reginald Frankenstein, called the pious Sister Monika " a pearl". Father Frankenstein was tightly connected to the history of the Institute, because for more than twenty years, he held retreats for our sisters, and he was also the spiritual teacher of the St. Magdalena monastery for some years. Sister Monika is now the postulant master, and she impresses upon them her deep beliefs with lecture and example.

Mother Hildegard Joeckle, Prioress 1910-1918

Most Reverend Mother Hildegard Joeckle, second Prioress of the Institute, was a noble character: a first-rate teacher and woman of silence. She was a master in expanding our new motherhouse to the inside: to strengthen the spirit of the Order. She died all too early in January of 1918.

Mother Alana Wagner

A new election made Sister M. Alana Wagner to our Prioress. An excellent teacher herself with deep knowledge and understanding, Mother Alana took all sisters' hearts by storm. She was full of good humor and her heart was filled with true motherly love. She especially took care of the sisters that were malnourished from the food deprivation during the war. Unfortunately, Mother Alana was severely ailing. She, who could have accomplished great deeds, died in June 1919, after only 1-1/2 years and deeply bemoaned by her sisters.

Mother Aquinata Steinfeltz

On the Feast of Holy Trinity of the year 1919, all of us gathered again for the election process, which designated Mother M. Aquinata Steinfeltz. Sister Aquinata had been a very proficient teacher at various schools, and she had been an especially competent teacher of Pedagogic for our own students at normal school. But she was destined for a higher profession. As Prioress of the Institute, her quest was for the deepening of the inner life. On that topic, she sent us her theological circulars on appropriate occasions – very stylish and rich in content.

But her work was especially characterized by her methods of teachers' training, following only the most modern requirements. She sent us sisters to University and to different European countries, to learn English and French. Also, the sisters' training in home economics and child care, needlework and nursing received Mother Aquinata's special attention. Because of numerous requests, Reverend Mother Ignatia – may God rest her soul – had added nursing to the already existing services of our institute.

Mother Aquinata's vision was such that she was immediately willing to send sisters to the Helena College on the Reverend Bishop Carroll's request.

This concludes Mother Bonaventura's excerpt of the Speyer history.

Acknowledgments

My immense thanks to Sylvia Goebel and Kathy Crissey for believing in this project and encouraging me to go forward. To Amy Nennemann who assisted me with the first steps and to Doug Williams for his friendship and invaluable support. And finally, to my son Heiko who always believed his mother would write a book.